REMARKS

UPON

ALCHEMY AND THE ALCHEMISTS,

INDICATING A METHOD OF DISCOVERING
THE TRUE NATURE OF

HERMETIC PHILOSOPHY;

AND SHOWING THAT THE SEARCH AFTER

The Philosopher's Stone

HAD NOT FOR ITS OBJECT THE DISCOVERY OF AN AGENT

FOR THE

TRANSMUTATION OF METALS.

BEING ALSO AN ATTEMPT TO RESCUE FROM UNDESERVED
OPPROBRIUM THE REPUTATION
OF A CLASS OF

EXTRAORDINARY THINKERS IN PAST AGES.

"Man shall not live by bread alone."

BOSTON:
CROSBY, NICHOLS, AND COMPANY,
111 WASHINGTON STREET.
1857.

Entered according to Act of Congress, in the year 1857, by
CROSBY, NICHOLS, AND COMPANY,
in the Clerk's Office of the District Court of the District of Massachusetts.

CAMBRIDGE:
METCALF AND COMPANY, PRINTERS TO THE UNIVERSITY.

PREFACE.

It may seem superfluous in the author of the following remarks to disclaim the purpose of reviving the study of Alchemy, or the method of teaching adopted by the Alchemists. Alchemical works stand related to moral and intellectual geography, somewhat as the skeletons of ichthyosauri and plesiosauri are related to geology. They are skeletons of thought in past ages.

It is chiefly from this point of view that the writer of the following pages submits his opinions upon Alchemy to the public. He is convinced that the character of the Alchemists, and the object of their study, have been almost universally misconceived; and as a matter of *fact*, though of the past, he thinks it of sufficient importance to take a step in the right direction for developing the true nature of the studies of that extraordinary class of thinkers.

The opinion has become almost universal, that

Alchemy was a "pretended science by which gold and silver were to be made by the transmutation of the baser metals into these substances, the agent of the transmutation being called the philosopher's stone." Those who professed this *Art* are supposed to have been either impostors or under a delusion created by impostors and mountebanks. This opinion has found its way into works on Science, and has been stereotyped in biographical dictionaries and in encyclopædias, large and small; and, in general, allusions to Alchemy, in histories, romances, and novels, are of but one character, and imply that the professors of the Art were either deluders or deluded, — were guilty of fraud or the victims of it.

It may be a hopeless task to announce a different persuasion with the expectation of superseding this deeply rooted prejudice; but the author thinks it a duty to declare the opinion he has derived from a careful reading of many alchemical volumes, and in the following remarks he has taken for his thesis the proposition that *Man* was the *subject* of Alchemy; and that the *object* of the Art was the perfection, or at least the improvement, of Man.

The salvation of man — his transformation from

evil to good, or his passage from a state of nature to a state of grace — was symbolized under the figure of the transmutation of metals. Under this point of view the works of the Alchemists may be regarded as treatises upon religious education, though they may now only serve to show past opinions upon this important subject.

The writings of the Alchemists are all symbolical, and under the words gold, silver, lead, salt, sulphur, mercury, antimony, arsenic, orpiment, sol, luna, wine, acid, alkali, and a thousand other words and expressions, infinitely varied, may be found the opinions of the several writers upon the great questions of God, nature, and man, all brought into or developed from one central point, which is Man, as the image of God.

The author is perfectly aware of the latitude of interpretation to which all symbolical writings are exposed, and that it is possible for an undisciplined imagination to make from such writings *anything* of *anything*, and indeed to make almost anything of *nothing*. He needs no schooling on this subject, but feels himself, on the contrary, in a position to justify his warning the readers of all symbolical works, that they cannot be too cautious and guarded against supplying from their own imaginations and afterthoughts, interpretations to all such works. They should hold themselves absolutely upon the immovable foundation of truth and nature, whereby alone they can save themselves from misapprehensions and from the danger of being carried entirely away from reality into mere dreams and fictions. But with the proper guards, supplied by sound theory and a knowledge of nature, it is extremely interesting, and the author thinks instructive, to interpret bygone forms of thought, even in alchemical volumes, in which it is quite possible that many precious jewels may be found, though the philosopher's stone be missed.

It would be a useless labor to enter here upon a defence of symbolic writing, when nothing is more certain than that men of genius in all ages, seemingly by a constraint of nature, have fallen into it. That the Sacred Scriptures are full of it must be confessed by all who are not in a condition to read as literal truth the history of Robinson Crusoe and of Gulliver's Travels;—not that the author would institute a comparison between these works and the sacred writings. He only means, by a reference to the Revelation, to the story of the man of Uz, to the beautiful parables of the

New Testament, &c., to show that teaching by way of similitude, parable, fable, allegory, or, in one word, by symbolism, is as old as writing itself.

While this form of teaching appears naturally to have been adopted by genius, from the earliest time, its preservation seems due to a corresponding working in the human mind, to which all symbolism is addressed. It is plain that, if a symbolic work finds no echo in the human heart, it must perish; while, for this very reason, where such works have been preserved through many ages, it affords a fair presumption that their authors have struck a vein of imperishable truth.

This species of writing is also the most innocent in the world, for the reason, that, while its literal sense is very frequently no sense at all, and is therefore harmless, its hidden sense, as intended by its author, must be equally harmless; for if the sense intended does not exist in nature, no counterpart is discoverable, and nothing permanent can come from it; while, if an echo is readily found, the symbolism must be true, — and all truth is valuable.

In the case of the Alchemists, who promised heaps of riches, it is admitted that multitudes of men were deluded by the mere literal reading of their works, or rather by their own absorbing desire of wealth. Such men were said, by the Alchemists, to have "the gold fever, which had darkened their senses." Men wholly bent on worldly treasures were rather the dupes of their own passions than deceived by the writings of the Alchemists, more especially since their writings are full of cautions against this very misunderstanding. The riches they promised were "the riches of the wisdom and knowledge of God" (Rom. xi. 33), and "of his grace" (Ephes. ii. 7).

The Alchemists were *Reformers* in their time, obliged indeed to work in secret, but nevertheless making their impression upon the public. They lived, for the most part, in an age when an open expression of their opinions would have brought them into conflict with the superstition of the time, and thus exposed them to the stake; — where, indeed, many of them perished, not having been sufficiently guarded in their language.

They were religious men when the spirit of religion was buried in forms and ceremonies, and when the priesthood had armed itself with the civil power to put down all opposition, and suppress all freedom, intellectual, civil, moral, and religious.

It was in that midnight of darkness that a light from heaven, as it seemed, was treated of, in books for the initiated, as the Elixir of Life, the Water of Life, the Universal Medicine, and the Philosopher's Stone.

The volumes in which this thought of the time was enshrined were written in symbolic form, to hide the subject from the crowd, not in a condition to profit by it, and to screen the authors from persecution. They are now measurably forgotten, and, the occasion of them having passed away, will never be revived and studied on their own account; but they yet exist for us and for future times as marvellous *skeletons*, where may be found abundant evidences that there were " giants in those days," though they made but little show in the world, living as they did in retirement, upon the " still, small voice," wherein lay chiefly their so much talked of secret.

In reading their works, with a knowledge of the historical position of the writers, one is strongly reminded of the query of Sir Thomas Browne. Who knows, says he, whether better men have not been forgot, than stand recorded in the book of time, who nevertheless may be registered in the book of God?

I have examined a great many alchemical works,

at a time of life and under circumstances when the imagination, if it ever deceived me, has "yielded its plumage," and I feel entirely able, as I am certainly willing, to see things as they are. I therefore say, after much study and deliberation, that the works of the *genuine* Alchemists, excluding those of ignorant imitators and mischievous impostors, are all essentially religious, and that the best external assistance for their interpretation may be found in a study of the Holy Scriptures, and chiefly in the New Testament, — that "light which was, before the light," being by no means, and on no account, overlooked.

There was no doubt an abundance of impostors who played upon the credulity and cupidity of the public, but the genuine Alchemists were religious men, who passed their time in legitimate pursuits, earning an honest subsistence, and in religious contemplations, studying how to realize in themselves the union of the divine and human nature, expressed in man by an enlightened submission to God's will; and they thought out and published, after a manner of their own, a method of attaining or entering upon this state, as the only rest of the soul.

The following little poem admirably "shadows" the life the adepts sought to reach: —

" There is an isle
Full, as they say, of good things; — fruits and trees
And pleasant verdure : a very master-piece
Of nature's ; where the men immortally
Live, following all delights and pleasures. There
Is not, nor ever hath been, Winter's cold
Or Summer's heat, the season still the same,—
One gracious Spring, where all, e'en those worst used
By fortune, are content. Earth willingly
Pours out her blessing : the words " thine " and " mine "
Are not known 'mongst them : all is common, free
From pain and jealous grudging. Reason rules,
Not fantasy : every one knows well
What he would ask of other ; every one
What to command : thus every one hath that
Which he doth ask ; what is commanded, does.
This island hath the name of Fortunate :
And, as they tell, is governed by a Queen
Well spoken and discreet, and therewithal
So beautiful, that, with one single beam
Of her great beauty, all the country round
Is rendered shining. When she sees arrive
(As there are many so exceeding curious
They have no fear of danger 'fore their eyes)
Those who come suing to her, and aspire
After the happiness which she to each
Doth promise in her city, she doth make
The strangers come together ; and forthwith,
Ere she consenteth to retain them there,
Sends for a certain season all to sleep.
When they have slept so much as there is need,
Then wake they them again, and summon them

Into her presence. There avails them not
Excuse or caution; speech however bland,
Or importunity of cries. Each bears
That on his forehead written visibly,
Whereof he hath been dreaming. They whose dreams
Have been of birds and hounds, are straight dismissed;
And at her royal mandate led away,
To dwell thenceforward with such beasts as these.
He who hath dreamed of sconces broken, war,
And turmoil, and sedition, glory won,
And highest feats achieved, is, in like guise,
An exile from her court; whilst one whose brow
Is pale, and dead, and withered, showing care
Of pelf and riches, she no less denies
To be his queen and mistress. None, in brief,
Reserves she of the dreamers in her isle,
Save him, that, when awakened he returns,
Betrayeth tokens that of her rare beauty
His dreams have been. So great delight hath she
In being and in seeming beautiful,
Such dreamer is right welcome to her isle.

All this is held a fable: but who first
Made and recited it hath, in this fable,
Shadowed a Truth."*

"The Philosophers," says Flammel, "have a garden, where the sun as well morning as evening remains with a most sweet dew, without ceas-

---

* *Heriot de Borderie*, (16th century,) translated by Cary.

ing, with which it is moistened; whose earth brings forth trees and fruits, which are transplanted thither, which also receive nourishment from the pleasant meadows. And this is done daily: and there they are corroborated and quickened, without ever fading; and this more in one year than in a thousand where the cold affects them."

Let an idea of the isle or garden gleam upon the soul as an attainable object, and the experience of that idea will explain much of the literature of past ages; especially such poems as the Romaunt of the Rose, translated by Chaucer. It may afford a hint in explanation of those *Love* Tales, the abuse of which style of writing brought out Cervantes; and, indeed, the large class of poems, as well as tales, excluding the base imitations, the counterfeit coin, known as the Love Literature of the Middle Ages, will find their interpretation in that idea, including the Sonnets and the Triumphs of Petrarch, and even the Divina Commedia itself.

If to yearn for such a life was folly, and is judged incompatible with the practical demands upon man living under the so-called curse of labor, it was at least an innocent folly, with which the world has never been overburdened; and the few who found, or thought they found, their rest in that Eden, may be pardoned by those who glory in what they call a more enlightened age. Even to seek it had a charm which smoothed the hardest external fate, as undoubtedly it supported many while suffering in the flames lighted by the Inquisition.

But, as I have elsewhere said, that Life is like an Art, which must be sought, if sought at all, for itself, and not for its rewards. Admission into the gardens of the Hesperides is accorded only to those whose "dreams" are exclusively upon the "beauty" of the presiding queen; for — and the reader may ponder on this principle — the success is contained in the dream itself, and is developed from it, just as every desire contains an essence of its own, which works itself into manifestation, whether it be good or whether it be evil; — but its quality is not to be estimated by what it accomplishes outwardly, but by what it deposits, that is, to use the language of Alchemy, by the *salt* it leaves in the soul where it originates.

I think proper to add, that my original design in preparing these Remarks was simply to express a mere opinion, and support it by a few citations from the works on Alchemy, and I thought a small pamphlet would answer this purpose. I have unexpectedly exceeded the size of a pamphlet, and find it necessary to go to press in a book form, though I did not aspire to "write a book." But although my appearance must be more formal than I intended, I desire to say that nothing original, as coming from myself, need be looked for in the volume. Whatever interest the work may have will be due to the class of men I have written about, who have furnished me with materials, and especially with extracts from their own writings, which I have been obliged to use freely in support of a simple opinion in regard to their labors and studies. This opinion, I am very sure, has some novelty to the present generation, and, if well founded, must then have some interest; though it may commend itself principally to speculative men who delight in a study but little regarded in our "practical age." But neither steam power nor telegraphs, with all their admitted wonders, themselves the product of the human mind, can ever destroy in man the tendency to search into the arcana of his own sublime and all but infinite nature, in whose "heart," as we read in the Holy Scriptures, God hath "set the world."

E. A. H.

St. Louis, Missouri, January, 1857.

REMARKS

UPON

ALCHEMY AND THE ALCHEMISTS.

SOME two years since, I printed a small pamphlet on the subject of Alchemy, my object being to throw out an idea with which I was strongly impressed, that the *Philosopher's Stone* was a mere symbol, and that the Alchemists were not in pursuit of gold, but of wisdom, carefully and conscientiously leaving the latter word undefined. The pamphlet was intended for the eye of my friends, and was not published or put on sale, though I was not unwilling to have it circulated among the curious who might be likely to look into the proposition I announced. It has been noticed in the Westminster Review for October, 1856, and the decision therein expressed, adverse to my view, has induced me to fortify my opinions by additional reasons, and by citations from alchemical works.

When I printed the pamphlet, I had read but a

few, some half a dozen, works on Alchemy, and my opinions were necessarily of a negative kind. I did not then, nor do I now, undertake to say precisely what the Alchemists sought. I was positive, however, that they were not in pursuit of gold or of worldly honors; and I am still of this opinion. I thought their object was religious, in which I am also fully confirmed by a further examination of alchemical works, of which I have obtained many since my pamphlet was printed.

I feel now somewhat better prepared to express an opinion upon their real object, though I wish to say, once for all, that the subject is still one of inquiry with me. I will endeavor, nevertheless, to state what I suppose they really sought, or at least the commencement of the work; yet I desire not to be considered as enlisting myself in defence of what I regard as the philosophy of those extraordinary writers.

But first I must say a word of the article in the Review. There is placed at the head of it the titles of three works, if my little pamphlet may be called one. The first is that of a French writer, Louis Figuier (1854), entitled *Alchemy and the Alchemists, or a Historical and Critical Essay upon Hermetical Philosophy.*

The second is that of a German, Dr. Herman Kopp (1843 – 44), entitled *The History of Chemistry*.

The third is that of my pamphlet, in which I express the opinion that the Philosopher's Stone is a mere symbol, signifying something which could not be expressed openly without incurring the danger of an *auto da fé*.

The title of the German work shows that the author must have taken up the subject of Alchemy only in its relation to chemistry; as perhaps its precursor, which it really was. He regarded Alchemy from the modern point of view of chemistry, and probably examined alchemical works for the purpose only of pointing out his opinion of the relation of Alchemy to the modern science of chemistry. In the prosecution of such a work, therefore, it is not to be supposed that the secret of the Alchemists, if they had one, would become recognizable, and all that can be expected from Dr. Kopp, in the premises, must be secondary and subordinate, so far as Alchemy is concerned. Yet I shall show that even Dr. Kopp, though writing professedly of chemistry and not of Alchemy, had some opinion bordering on the truth in regard to the real object of the latter, though he did not choose to explain it at length, because his proper subject, Chemistry, did not require it.

Pass now to M. Figuier, and it must be observed that the Reviewer expresses the opinion very decidedly that the French writer, though he enlarges upon the title of the German author, has nevertheless drawn all of his materials from the laborious German, comparing him to a *parasite* living upon the vitality of the massy German.

Upon this state of the case, as we have no right to expect a treatise upon Alchemy from the German, much less can we look for such a treatise in the French work.

But this is not all; the writer in the Review very candidly and honestly admits, that, in the preparation of his article, he has depended upon the Frenchman and the German; so that what was not even wine in the original is twice diluted in the Westminster Review article.

In short, the writer of the article knows nothing of the Alchemists from an examination of their works, and takes his opinions from others; from a Frenchman who drew his materials from a German, and a German who did not treat of Alchemy except incidentally to his subject, the *History of Chemistry*.

Nothing further need be said to show that neither the article in the Review nor the French work can furnish any satisfactory information upon the subject of Alchemy.

To refer now more especially to the work of M. Figuier, which is before me, I observe that all of his citations from alchemical works, to illustrate the alleged extravagance and absurdity of their authors, are expressly credited to Dr. Kopp in these remarkable words: " *Maintenant, ajoute M. Kopp, à qui nous empruntons les citations precedents, si l'on entend par monde le microcosm que l'homme represente, l'interpretation sera facile.*"

How could the French author overlook the plain signification of this remarkable passage, in which Dr. Kopp says expressly, that, by considering *the world as the microcosm which man represents, it would be easy to interpret the writings of the Alchemists*, or at least the citations made by himself to exhibit their opinions or mode of procedure? But the French writer takes no notice of this admission of the German, so honorable to his penetration, but proceeds immediately to characterize the Alchemists as guilty of " deplorable aberrations, the product of a delirious imagination, the disorders of which exceed all power of analysis."

The English Reviewer also overlooks the pregnant hint of the German, and, throwing himself into the arms of the Frenchman, quotes at third hand a number of passages, detached from their proper connection, for the purpose of showing up the absurdity of the philosophical stone seekers, absolutely blind as to their real object.

Leaving, therefore, the French writer and the Reviewer to feed upon the fragments they have elected to deal with, I take up the citation from Dr. Kopp, and will endeavor to substantiate the accuracy of his hint, and show that the Alchemists, in all their writings, had Man in view, regarding him as a microcosm, or miniature of the great world; or, as they are fond of quoting, as the Image of God, in the language of Moses.

My proposition is, that the *subject* of Alchemy was *Man;* while the *object* was the perfection of Man, which was supposed to centre in a certain unity with the Divine nature.

All of the Alchemists, so far as I have examined their writings, might place in the "fore-front" of their works a number of the most enlightening passages from Scripture, as indicating their doctrines and objects; among them the following, which I will recite at large, to save the trouble of a reference, and I will copy them with some general view to the order of the "great work," as the Alchemists call their Art.

"Blessed are they which do hunger and thirst after righteousness: for they shall be filled."

"Blessed are the poor in spirit: for theirs is the kingdom of heaven."

"Blessed are the pure in heart: for they shall see God."

"I say unto thee, except a man be born again" ("from above," in the margin), "he cannot see the kingdom of God."

"The wind bloweth where it listeth, and thou hearest the sound thereof, but canst not tell whence it cometh, and whither it goeth: so is every one that is born of the Spirit."

"Neither shall they say, Lo here! or, Lo there! for, behold, the kingdom of God is within you."

"I and my Father are one."

"..... as thou, Father, art in me, and I in thee, that they [the disciples] also may be one in us; ..... I in them, and thou in me, that they may be made perfect in one."

"Give not that which is holy unto the dogs, neither cast ye your pearls before swine, lest they trample them under their feet, and turn again and rend you."

"And with many such parables spake he the word unto them, as they were able to hear it. But without a parable spake he not unto them [the people]; and when they were alone, he expounded all things to his disciples."

"The fear of the Lord is the beginning of wisdom."

"Happy is the man that findeth wisdom, and the man that getteth understanding: for the merchandise of it is better than the merchandise of silver, and the gain thereof than fine gold. She is more precious than rubies: and all the things thou canst desire are not to be compared unto her. Length of days is in her right hand; and in her left hand riches and honor.

"Her ways are ways of pleasantness and all her paths are peace. She is a tree of life to them that lay hold upon her; and happy is every one that retaineth her.

"The Lord by wisdom hath founded the earth; by understanding hath he established the heavens. ..... My son, let them not depart from thine eyes; keep sound wisdom and discretion. So shall they be life unto thy soul and grace to thy neck."

"Get wisdom, get understanding; forget it not: neither decline from the words of my mouth. Forsake her not, and she shall preserve thee: love her, and she shall keep thee."

"Keep thy heart with all diligence; for out of it are the issues of life."

"A wise man will hear and will increase learning; and a man of understanding shall attain unto wise counsels; to understand a proverb, and the interpretation, the words of the wise, and their dark sayings."

All of these sayings are perfectly congenial to the Alchemist, and exactly in harmony with his object.

But an important point must here be explained without reserve, it being necessary to a right understanding of the true position of the Alchemists; especially in what have been called the Dark Ages, when there was neither political nor religious toleration.

The Address to the Reader, in the English copy of Sandivogius, opens in this strain:—

"There is abundance of Knowledge, yet but little Truth known. The generality of our knowledge is but as castles in the air, or groundless fancies. I know but of two ways that are ordained for getting of Wisdom, viz. the Book of God and the Book of Nature; and these also, but as they are read with reason. Many look upon the former as a thing below them; upon the latter, as a ground of Atheism, and therefore neglect both. It is my judgment, that as to search the Scriptures is most necessary, so without reason it is impossible to understand them. Faith without reason is but implicity. If I cannot understand by reason *how* a thing is, yet I will see *that* a thing is so, before I will believe it to be so. I will ground my believing of the Scripture upon Reason; I will improve my Reason by Philosophy. How shall we convince gainsayers of the truth of the Scriptures, but by principles of Reason?

"When God made Man after his own Image, how was that? Was it not by making him a rational creature? Men therefore that lay aside reason, in the reading of sacred mysteries, do but *un-man* themselves, and become further involved in a labyrinth of errors. Hence it is that their Religion is degenerated into irrational notions.

"Now, to say that *pure* Philosophy is *true* Divinity, will haply seem a paradox [in 1650]; yet if any one should affirm it, he would not be Heterodox.

"When Job had been a long time justifying himself against God, — which I conceive was by reason of his ignorance of God and himself, — God undertakes to convince him of his error by the principles of Nature; and this, to bring him to the knowledge of both; as may be seen at large, Job xxxviii.

"Can any one affirm that Hermes, Plato, Aristotle, (though pure Naturalists,) were not most deep Divines? Do not all grant that the two first chapters of *Genesis* are true Divinity? I dare affirm that they are the most deep and the truest Philosophy. Yea, they are the ground and sum of all Divinity, and Philosophy; and if rightly understood, will teach thee more knowledge of *God*, and of *thyself*, than all the books in the world besides."

From such passages as the above, or those of a similar import, abundantly found in the works of the Alchemists, I cannot but say that they sought the Truth upon evidences drawn from the nature of things, and received it only for itself; and were influenced in its reception by neither tradition nor authority.

With the Alchemists in Christian countries, the doctrines of Christ were received as true in themselves, or in the nature of things, and *therefore* were believed to have been announced by Christ; but they were not regarded as true simply upon the ground that Christ announced them. With them, the "wisdom of the doctrine established the truth of Christianity, and not miracles." The Alchemists would have the lovers of their art test all doctrines by what they call "the possibility of Nature." Hence the test of doctrine was not with them a written record; and, consistently with this principle, no Alchemist urges his opinions upon authority, but always in the style of "My son, listen to my words"; but he adds, *Prove them;* or, he might say, with St. Paul, — one of the most zealous, bold, and independent reformers the world ever saw, — "Prove all things, but hold fast that which is good."

Notwithstanding this high authority, he who accepts truth only because it may be proved, or proved to be "good," and disregards mere authority, is commonly stigmatized as an infidel.

The Alchemists, therefore, standing upon this ground, would have been persecuted had they published their opinions openly; for they lived, for the most part, at a period when it was supposed by those in authority, that coercion and violence might be legitimately employed to *force* men into the established public faith, the imagined enemies of which, besides being held up to public abhorrence, were often burned at the stake. Allusions to this state of things frequently occur in the writings of the Alchemists, as in *The Open Way to the Shut Palace of the King*, where the author says:

"I dare affirm that I do possess more riches than the whole known world is worth; but cannot make use thereof, because of the snares of knaves." The true explanation of this allusion to riches is in Matt. xvi. 26, for Eyrenæus proceeds: "I disdain, I loathe, I detest this idolizing of gold and silver, by the price whereof the pomp and vanities of the world are celebrated. Ah, filthy evil! ah, vain nothingness! Believe ye that I conceal these things out of envy? No, surely; for I protest to thee that I grieve from the very bottom of my soul, that we are driven as it were like outcasts from the face of the Lord throughout the earth. We travel through many nations, just like vagabonds, and dare not take upon ourselves the care of a family, neither do we possess any fixed habitation. And although we possess all things, yet can we use but a few. What, therefore, are we happy in, excepting speculation and meditation only, wherein we meet with great satisfaction of mind? Many do believe (that are strangers to the Art) that, if they should enjoy it, they would do such and such things; so also even we did formerly believe, but being grown more wary, by the hazard we have run, *we have chosen a more secret method.* For whosoever hath once escaped imminent peril of his life, he will (believe me) become more wise for the time to come." Yet he exclaims: "My heart murmureth things unheard of; my spirit beats in my breast for the good of all Israel. . . . . . Would to God that every ingenious man, in the whole earth, understood this science! . . . . . Then would virtue, naked as it is, be held in great honor, merely for its own amiable nature." But he adds: "*Our gold* is not to be bought for money, though you should offer a crown or a kingdom for it; for it is the gift of God."

As the intolerance of the Middle Ages is a familiar fact, known to every one, I have no disposition to dwell upon it; and have referred to it only to assign it as one cause of the esoteric writing of the Alchemists. They communicated with each other by symbols, writing of salt, sulphur, mercury, &c., and of the transmutation of metals, by which they saved their own heads, though they plunged hundreds and thousands of the "profane" into vain and useless efforts to find a *tangible* agent for turning the baser metals into gold. "Who is to blame," says one of them, "*the Art*, or those who seek it upon false principles?"

Another reason for their obscure mode of writing

was of a higher order, and it was this: that, as most men were educated in religious tenets according to tradition, without understanding the true grounds of the doctrines imposed upon them, it was not considered safe to shake the hold of the tradition by proposing a new rule of conduct, not easily apprehended. In plain words, it was believed to be better for society that men should be held to their duty by hope and fear, than be exposed to injury by a misunderstood doctrine of freedom; for man is not free by denying the false, but by living in the truth. "The truth shall make you free," was the doctrine of Alchemy, as well as of the Gospel.

With the Alchemists, the ancient saying, KNOW THYSELF, inscribed upon the Temple of Apollo (attributed by some to Pythagoras, by others to the Egyptians), as an injunction, was the ground and sum of all wisdom. In this knowledge was found, as they believed, the knowledge of God; not that God is in man except as he is in all things, but the *knowledge of God* lies in the nature of man, and not in the nature of any other thing in the universe. He who looks for it elsewhere, is on a journey away from the object he seeks, and shall be disappointed. This I regard as the opinion of the Alchemists.

I know of no one among that class of writers who has stated the ground of their proceedings more distinctly than Van Helmant, where he says: —

"Seeing that the Creator of all beings, before the foundation of the world, and before ever they were brought forth, had and contained the same in his Mind and Wisdom, — even the little world [man, the microcosm] as well as the greater, according to the testimony of Scripture [here he quotes passages from Scripture], — must not then the world, the greater [the macrocosm] as well as the lesser, have their Creator, as their original and beginning, within themselves, so that neither the Creator nor his creature are separate from each other? . . . . . Seeing, then, that it cannot be said that perfection is attained, before the end hath reached its beginning, and the beginning united itself with the end, in order to a new birth and production, the question is, whether both the greater and the lesser world, in order to reach perfection, must not, in all their workings, aim at this, viz. that they may return to their beginning, to be united with it."

Again: "Seeing, then, that all the creatures of God, in order to their melioration and glorification, stand in an endless revolution, in order to perfection, and yet must be known and comprehended; and seeing that a thing cannot be known otherwise than by its end and operation, or outworking, as a tree by its fruits; and that the lesser world is the end and comprisal of all creatures and works of God, and consequently an out-birth of the great world, wherein all other creatures are comprised; the question then is, Whether there can be any other way by which man may attain to a right knowledge of the great world, with and in all its parts, than *in and out of himself;* especially since in him, as in the end and abridgment of all things, the Beginning hath manifested itself; — for the End is nothing but a Beginning wrought out, that is, displayed into act and manifested; so that the End is hid in the Beginning, as the Beginning is manifested in the End? And whether, as a consequence of this, both the worlds have not a great affinity, and perfect likeness, yea, and *unity one with the other;* and whether they must not be wrought out with one another, and thereby reach their highest perfection?"

Alchemical volumes are filled with intimations of the *mystery* involved in the nature of man; thus Weidenfeld exclaims: —

" Very great and incomprehensible gifts hath

the most High God vouchsafed us; in the acknowledgment of which it is our duty both day and night to love, worship, and revere him with our whole heart, and everywhere extol his name with all our might; for besides his creating us out of nothing, and redeeming us with his most precious blood, he hath also made us partakers of all the blessings contained in the greater world; for which reason *Man* is called *Microcosm;* for it has by divine inspiration been revealed to us that the virtues of all things, animal, vegetable, and mineral, are in *Man.*"

The English translator of a work said to have been written in Arabic, by Alipili, entitled *Centrum Naturæ Concentratum, or the Salt of Nature Regenerated,* in his Address to "the Reader," says:—

" The highest wisdom consists in this, for Man to know Himself, because in him God has placed his eternal Word, by which all things were made and upheld, to be his Light and Life, by which he is capable of knowing all things both in time and eternity...... Therefore let the high inquirers and searchers into the deep mysteries of nature learn first to know what they have in themselves, before they seek in foreign matters without them; and by the divine power within them, let them first heal themselves and TRANSMUTE their own souls; then they may go on prosperously, and seek with good success the mysteries and wonders of God in all natural things."

This is but a reflection from what is found in the text of the volume in these words: —

"He that hath the knowledge of the *Microcosm*, cannot long be ignorant of the knowledge of the Macrocosm. This is that which the Egyptian industrious searchers of Nature so often said, and loudly proclaimed,— that every one should KNOW HIMSELF. This speech their dull disciples [meaning the Greeks] took in a moral sense, and in ignorance affixed it to their Temples. But I admonish thee, whosoever thou art, that desirest to dive into the inmost parts of Nature, if that which thou seekest thou findest not within thee, *thou wilt never find it without thee.* If thou knowest not the excellency of thine own house, why dost thou seek and search after the excellency of other things? The universal Orb of the world contains not so great mysteries and excellences as *a little Man, formed by God to his own Image.* And he who desires the primacy amongst the Students of Nature, will nowhere find a greater or better field of study than Himself. Therefore will I here follow the example of the *Egyptians*, and from my whole heart, and certain true experience proved by me, speak to my neighbor in the words of the Egyptians, and with a loud voice do now proclaim: O MAN, KNOW THYSELF; *in thee is hid the Treasure of Treasures.*"

The author then falls into the conventional mystic language about the central salt, the firmament, the astrum, the spiritual water, the watery spirit, the water of life, etc., etc., which would not be pertinent here, the point now in question requiring me only to show that *Man* is the *Subject* of Alchemy. Other points will arise in their due place.

Sandivogius, one of the most universally acknowledged *adepts*, speaks in the following manner of the *mysteries* involved in the nature of Man:—

" The most high Creator was willing to manifest all natural things unto Man, wherefore he showed to us that celestial things themselves were naturally made, by which his absolute and incomprehensible Power and Wisdom might be so much the more freely acknowledged; all which things the Philosophers [meaning the Alchemists], in the Light of Nature, as in a Looking-glass, have a clear sight of. For which cause they esteemed highly of this Art [of Alchemy], viz. not so much out of covetousness for gold or silver, but for knowledge sake, not only of all natural things, but also of the power of the Creator; but they were willing to speak of these things only sparingly and figuratively, lest the Divine Mysteries by which Nature is illustrated should be discovered to the unworthy; which *thou*, [reader,] *if thou knowest how to* KNOW THYSELF, and art not of a stiff neck, mayest easily comprehend, created as thou art in the likeness of the great world, *yea, after the Image of God.* . . . . . Thou, therefore, that desirest to attain to this Art, in the first place, put thy whole trust in God thy Creator, and urge him by thy prayers, and then assuredly believe that he will not forsake thee; for if God shall know that thy Heart is *sincere*, and that thy whole trust is put in him, he will, by one means or another, shew thee a way, and assist thee in it, and thou shalt obtain thy desire. The Fear of the Lord is the beginning of wisdom. Pray, but yet work: God indeed gives understanding, but thou must know how and when to use it."

Cornelius Agrippa, an Alchemist, and, like many other great men, misunderstood in his day, writes:—

" There is one thing by God created [he does not name it, but he means man], the subject of all wonderfulness in earth and in heaven; it is actually animal, vegetable, and mineral; found everywhere, known [properly] by few, by none expressed by his proper name, but hid in numbers, figures, and riddles, without which neither alchemy, nor natural magic, can attain their perfect end."

Thomas Norton, a very old writer on Alchemy of great authority (of the fifteenth century), wrote his "Ordinall" in verse, and tells all but the very blind the real *subject* of the Art in these words: —

> "Noble authors, men of glorious fame,
> Called our STONE *Microcosmus* by name:
> For his composition is withouten doubt,
> Like to this *world* in which we walk about:
> Of Heat, of Cold, of Moist, and of Dry,
> Of Hard, of Soft, of Light, and of Heavy,
> Of Rough, of Smooth, and of things stable,
> Mingled with things fleeting and movable;
> Of all kinds contrary brought to one accord,
> Knit by the doctrine of God by our blessed Lord.
> Whereby of *Metals* is made transmutation,
> Not only in color [appearance] but transubstantiation,
> In which ye have need to know this thing,
> How all the virtues of the elements transmuting,
> Upon the transmuted must have full domination,
> Before that the substance be in transmutation;
> And all parts transmuted must figured be,
> In the elements transmuting impressed by degree.
> So that the third thing elemented of them all

>Of such condition ever more be shall ;
>That it truly have, it may be none other,
>But her substance of that one, and her virtue of that other."

A friend remarks at my elbow, that this is "poetry under difficulties," which is very true; but it is not cited for its beauty, but in testimony to a fact.

In as clear a manner, George Ripley declares the *subject* of the *Stone* in the following lines: —

>"For as of one mass was made all thing,
>Right so must it in our practice be,
>All our Secrets of one Image must spring :
>In Philosophers' books therefore who wishes may see,
>Our *Stone* is called the *less-world*, one and three."

That is, the Stone is Man, of one nature, — of body, soul, and spirit.

In the Dialogue of *Arislaus*, published in the *Alchemists's Enchiridion*, in 1672, *man* is indicated as the Stone in this language: —

"Now in this discourse will I manifest to thee the natural condition of the Stone of the Philosophers, apparelled with a triple garment, even this Stone of Riches and Charity, the Stone of Relief from Languishment;—in which is contained every secret; being a Divine Mystery and Gift of God, than which there is nothing in this world more sublime.

"Therefore diligently observe what I say, viz.

that 't is apparelled with a *Triple garment*, that is to say, with a *Body*, *Soul*, and *Spirit*."

Any one having the least acquaintance with these works would recognize the *subject* of the author by this language, and that it is *Man*.

In the sequel I shall adduce many other evidences in confirmation of this point, to wit, that all the books of Alchemy treat of *Man;* and they treat of no other thing in the universe except in its relation to *Man;* but never, when treating of the mysteries of the Art, by this proper name.

Man is the central object in all alchemical books; yet, not man as he is an individual, but as he is a *Nature*, containing or manifesting the great world, or as he is the Image of God.

Whoever desires to understand anything of Alchemy must carry this idea along with him in reading works on the subject; and then, however much he may dissent from the principles or pretensions of the *Art*, he may form some comprehension of the use made by this class of writers of the symbolic words, salt, sulphur, mercury, sol, luna, etc.; and under these or other similar names may be discovered, if any one thinks it worth while, what the writers thought of God, Nature, and Man, or Man, Nature, and God, — one and three, three and one.

Although the writers represent Man by an endless variety of names, as representing the true Proteus, they most commonly speak of him as a *Metal* or *Mineral*; hence one says: —

"Minerals have their roots in the air, their heads and tops in the earth. Our Mercury is aerial; look for it, therefore, in the air and the earth."

In this passage, *Minerals* and *our Mercury* refer to the same thing, and it is the *subject* of Alchemy, the Stone; and we may remember that Plato defined or described *Man* as a growth having his root in the air, his tops in the earth. Man walks indeed upon the surface of the earth, as if nothing impeded his vision of heaven; but he walks nevertheless at the bottom of the atmosphere, and between these two, his *root* in the air, he must work out his salvation.

Another writer says: "Minerals made of *living* mercury and *living* sulphur [Soul and Body], are to be chosen; work with them sweetly, not with haste and precipitancy."

Again: "Those that know the mercury and sulphur of the Philosophers, know that they are made of pure gold and the finest luna and argent vive [Soul, Body, and Spirit, considered essentially], which are daily seen, and looked upon, from which our argent vive is elicited."

"The work," says one, "while yet crude, is called our water permanent, our lead, our Saturn, our Jupiter; when better decocted, then it is argent, then magnesia, and white sulphur; when it is red, it is called auripigment, coral, gold, ferment, or stone, a lucid water of celestial color."

"Our Stone," says another, "in the beginning is called water; when the Body is dissolved, air or wind; when it tends to consolidation, then it is named earth; and when it is perfect and fixed, it is called *fire*."

Again: "Although the wise men have varied their names and perplexed their sayings, yet they would always have us think but of one only thing, one disposition, one way. The wise men know this one thing; and that it is one they have often proved."

This one thing is, first, Man, as a *Nature;* one, essentially or substantially;—but when the writers refer to man phenomenally, they speak of him under different names indicating different states, as he is before or after "purification"; or they refer to his Body, his Soul, or his Spirit under different names. Sometimes they speak of the whole man as mercury, or by some other name, and then by the same word perhaps they speak of something special as "*our* mercury," which has besides a multitude of other names.

By *our* mercury, *our* sulphur, etc., they mean the philosopher's mercury, and not the common mineral.

I am not defending this mode of writing, but I affirm that the whole subject of Alchemy is Man. But each writer, for the most part, designates him by a word of his own choosing; hence one writes of *Antimony*, another of *Lead*, another of *Zinc*, another of *Arsenic*, etc., etc. Men are designated most frequently by the metals, but these are often called by astronomical names, as *Jupiter, Saturn, Mars*, etc., the best men, by nature, being likened to gold, and inferior men to the inferior metals.

Although men are of diverse dispositions and tempers, some being angelic and others satanic, yet the Alchemists insist with St. Paul that "all the nations of men are of one blood"; that is, of one *nature*, and that in man by which he is one nature it is the special object of Alchemy to bring into life and action, by means of which, if it could universally prevail, mankind would be constituted into a brotherhood.

This is properly the "mercury of the Philosophers," and this is what is referred to when M. Figuier, quoting the Alchemists, says: "*La seule difficulté, dans la preparation de la pierre philosophale, consiste donc à obtenir le mercure des philosophes.*" He goes on to say, speaking of the theory, yet supposing an agent for transmuting metals is the object, that, this mercury once found, the work is easy, — a work for "women and children." He adds, still quoting the Alchemists, that this work is no slight undertaking; that all the Alchemists acknowlege it to be a work above human power, and that it can be obtained only by the grace of God, or by the friendship of an adept to whom it has been revealed. He says it is called *animated mercury, double mercury, mercury twice born, the green lion, the serpent, sharp water, vinegar, virgin's milk*, etc.; but he adds, speaking now for himself, *that none of the Alchemists have ever discovered it.*

With due deference to M. Figuier, I expect to show that this *mercury* is no other than a perfectly pure conscience, or a conscience purified under a sense of the presence of God; and the "difficulty" of *discovering* it is the difficulty of *exciting* or rousing it in the breast of man, in order to his improvement.

I would put it to any experienced man, or especially teacher of youth or guide of those more advanced in life, whether the whole difficulty, and therefore the whole *Art* in improving man, is not in establishing in his bosom a permanent, enduring sense of absolute right, and an undeviating purpose of being governed by it. It is one of the most difficult things in the world to take a man in what is called his natural state, St. Paul's natural man, after he has been for years in the indulgence of all of his passions, having a view to the world, to honors, pleasures, wealth, and make him sensible of the mere abstract claims of right, and willing to relinquish one single passion in deference to it. Most assuredly this is the one grand task of teachers; but this once accomplished, the work of improvement is easy and may very properly be said to be "children's play."

Consider a man ever seeking only what may gratify some selfish passion, a stranger to all generous impulses, unconscious perhaps of their existence, or only regarding their manifestation in others as evidence of imbecility and weakness; how is such a man to be brought out of this state into a better view of things, so as to feel his dependence upon others, and appreciate their claims upon him?

Take a man whose soul is corrupted by all sorts of bad passions, until he has become morbidly sensitive in everything that in any manner interferes with his personal comfort; let him be petulant, irritable, and morose;— how is such a man to be improved?

I might speak of downright sins, which generate a class of men, a few of whom find their temporal homes in prisons and penitentiaries, or expiate their crimes upon the gallows; how are such men to be stopped in their career, and brought to a sense of duty?

Undoubtedly the great "difficulty" in all these cases is to bring into action the philosophical *mercury;* that is, to awaken the conscience, which lies buried in them; but though buried and inactive, "it is not dead, but sleepeth."

Take another class more numerous than any other,— those who are distracted between contrary passions, such as a love of pleasure and a love of money, or a love of glory and a love of ease. What peace can such people have, or how is it possible for them to enjoy tranquillity? They need a complete revolution of character or disposition. So with those who, under a vague notion of being in the right, having no more solid foundation for it than self-conceit, — who think the whole world wrong but themselves, and are uneasy and unhappy with everything around them which does not happen to be adjusted to their particular wishes and predilections. Such people often look with an evil eye upon Providence, which, somehow, proceeds to its general ends in total disregard of all incongruous individualities. How are such people to be dealt with? To tell them plainly that they are in error, is only to arouse their enmity and excite opposition; but create in them the philosophical mercury, — set their conscience on fire, — and the remedy is at hand; but to do this is the great "difficulty." Who doubts this but those who are in need of this same mercury?

There are no people in the world so suspicious and sensitive as those who are in error. They are like porcupines; you cannot approach them without danger, and truly do the Alchemists refer to these various kinds of people under such names as *arsenic, vitriol, vipers,* etc., and yet in all these substances, as well as in *Antimony, Lead,* and a thousand other things, they seek for a certain mercury, which itself has as many names as the substances in which it is found; as, oil, vinegar, honey, wormwood, etc.; and yet this same mercury is considered as one only unalterable thing. It is called an incombustible sulphur, because in whomsoever the conscience is properly awakened, a fire is raised which burns and consumes everything opposed to its own nature.

If any one doubts this, let him study the nature of the conscience, and see how uncompromising it is; that it can neither be bribed nor hoodwinked; that it is ubiquitous, and is everywhere present with its subject. Of the conscience it may be truly said, Whither can a man go to escape from it, or how can a man flee from its presence? if he ascend up into heaven, it is there; and if he makes his bed in hell, it is there also. If once roused, it can in no manner be quieted and put to rest but by an unreserved and unqualified submission; but then, though it had pursued its victim as an avenging fire, the moment it attains its legitimate supremacy it unfolds its healing virtues and becomes an assuaging balm, a *sovereign medicine*, — the medicine of the Alchemists, — the only true Æsculapius of a " wounded spirit."

A study of the conscience may furnish us something of a key to the ancient Stoic doctrine, that *Pain is not an Evil;* for it is not said that pain is not pain by saying that it is not evil. The only evil in the world is a self-condemnation, or a condemnation of one's own conscience. Pain, as such, does not suppose this, and is in its own nature transient. It may be mitigated or removed by the skill of a physician; or, if it terminates in the death of the body, this is a simple, natural event, and has no necessary connection with the conscience, and is therefore not an evil under the definition assumed. Then, with regard to the evil of a self-condemnation, this is so far from being absolutely evil, that it is universally adjudged to be a sign of some true life in the moral system, which needs only due management to revive and fortify the subject of it.

From this view, the worst evil, that is, the worst condition in life, is one in which the conduct is irregular, under a sleeping conscience, the *patient* suffering nothing for the time being, though his course of life may be daily "heaping up wrath against the day of wrath."

As a protection against this condition, nature seems to have provided a *tendency to fear* imaginary and even impossible evils, having various names, which, it is said, "ought not to be mentioned to polite ears."

It will be remembered that a healthy action of the conscience always precedes the contemplated deed, and this it is which establishes the specific difference between regret and remorse, and constitutes the true evil of the deed; and it is independent of both its pains and its pleasures, which, in respect to the conscience, are merely contingent, accidental, and temporal.

The conscience is a study by itself. The Alchemists often speak of it as in a "crude" state, as common mercury (not that which they call *our* mercury), when in many men it is hardly recognizable, and its possessor is scarcely conscious that he has such a companion, which nevertheless is the witness of all that is done. In this state its possessor is in danger of temporarily mistaking for it some transient passion, as a love of money, or of reputation; as where a question of *right* is settled by the influence of personal wishes or the love of applause.

But this is not the true philosophical mercury, which is the sense of right acting under the consciousness of the presence of God, when all deceits and equivocations become of no avail, and the soul is compelled to sit in judgment upon itself. This is the commencement of that internal reformation of character which will endure, and flame up all the brighter, under trials. To bring about this reformation *according to nature*, and *not by violence*, is one great object of the Alchemists.

Yet this is but an entrance upon what is called the "great work," the *End* of which it is not my purpose to speak of at length. I say that this is the way to the philosopher's stone; but the End "is not yet."

What one principle is it, more than any other, that confines the extravagances and wanderings of the *Race* within definite limits, so that each age in history recognizes itself in every other? It is not *reason*, however strongly this is claimed as the distinguishing endowment of man, but it is the *sense of right*, that is, conscience. This makes itself felt all the more by the wrongs of all sorts which mark the pages of history. It is this principle, the principle or sense of *right*, well or ill understood, which lies at the foundation of all international law, and theoretically determines all national controversies. All questions between independent nations are theoretically decided by the same principle that disposes of controversies between any two of the humblest individuals. In national quarrels vast results, of course, depend upon mere power; but the moral sense of the world is not thereby overcome, and in all cases the impartial historian, in his own sense of right, appeals to this same sense in the race, and fixes the moral judgment of mankind upon all national acts.

All laws, also, in civilized states, are theoretically based upon the sense of the *just*, and aim at the security of *right*. Juries are impanelled to do *justice*; that is, to discover and enforce *right*. In short, throughout society, in every phase and department of it, whether on a large or a small scale, whatever is *wrong* instantly arouses the sense of *right*, with a disposition to establish it. Efforts are then made in some shape or other to rectify the wrong, and reason is but an humble aid employed to find out and apply the remedy. How far the right end is attained in the *disposition* to attain it, may be a question worthy of a Socrates to discuss.

This sense of right is what the Alchemists call an immaterial, incorruptible, and inextinguishable *Fire*, which, Pontanus says, " is a matter mineral, equal, continuous, vapors or fumes not, unless too much provoked; partakes of sulphur [as the jargon runs, meaning a celestial spirit], and is taken otherwise than from matter; it destroys all things, dissolves, congeals, coagulates, and calcines, — is adapted to penetrate, — and is a compendium without any great cost." It *transmutes*, but "is not itself transmuted with the matter, because it is nothing of the matter."

Now, when the *conscience*, wherein the sense of right and justice has existence, becomes active under the *idea of God*, it is endowed with supernatural force, and is then, as I understand it, the Alchemist's philosophical mercury: it is also his salt of mercury: it is no less his sovereign *Treacle*, of which much may be read in their books, though of a kind quite unlike that of a justly celebrated novelist of the day. This is also the *Salt of Tartar*, of which we read in alchemical works: it is also the *Spirit of Wine*, " driven to the centre by cold," but not thereby destroyed; on the contrary, it is only made more piercing and active, though the removal of the *envelope* may need an *external fire;* for we read in these books of one, two, three, and four fires. This is also the *Viperine Salt* described with wonderful properties, and said to have an *oil* of marvellous qualities; — as we may read in a work with the following curious *hermetic* title: "*New Experiments upon Vipers; containing also an exact description of all the parts of a Viper, the seat of his poison, and the several effects thereof; together with the exquisite remedies that by the skilful may be drawn from Vipers for the cure of their bitings as well as for other maladies.*"

This work (of man) was originally written in French, but was published in English in 1670.

"The Volatile Salt of Vipers," says this writer, "is to be considered *as a Sun,* as well among the parts that rise by distillation, as among those that rest in the retort; there being none among those that are come over, but have borrowed from it all the virtue it can have; nor any of those that remain, but have need of it, or are useless without it." These writers often speak of man as a *retort,* an *alembic,* a *cucurbit,* in which *fermentation* takes place and thoughts are *distilled.* He is sometimes called a *furnace,* a name also applied to great nature itself, the great furnace. "The phlegm," the author continues, "that rises first, carries always some part with it, without which it would produce no effect. That which is called Spirit is nothing else, to speak aright, but a volatile salt, which in the distillation hath been followed by a little *phlegm* dissolving it and giving it the form of a spirit; which may be shown by the *rectification,* wherein that saline volatile part is separated, raised, and coagulated into a *white* and crystalline form, and leaveth at the bottom of the cucurbit the moisture that had changed its nature, and is nothing else but phlegm. We say on this occasion the same thing of what many authors improperly call the volatile spirit of the human skull [?], of hartshorn, and of other parts of animals, they being nothing else but volatile salts mixed with phlegm, which they afterwards quit, *when they are rectified.* ..... The terrestrial part hath nothing in it that deserves to be considered, and it may justly be called *Terra mortua,* dead earth, after it is freed from its fixed salt. [Some of the writers called it *Terra damnata.*] So that all the parts that rise by distillation, as well as those that cannot rise, are of small force or altogether useless, without the volatile salt. It is therefore upon good reason that we attribute to it the principal virtues which a Viper [?] can furnish."

To point out the medicinal action of this salt, this writer says: " The similitude of substance which the *Volatile Salt of Viper* hath with the spiritous part of our body, conjoined to its subtle and piercing quality, is the reason, that, accommodating itself to their condition, and finding all liberty for its action [by the removal of "superfluities" to be hereafter explained], it produceth all the effects it is capable of, [that is, under given conditions it does all it *can*,] and penetrates without any opposition into the most secret and the most remote parts of the body. It hath this peculiar property, that though it acts as a sovereign, and finds nothing of resistance to its dominion, yet it exerts it not as a conqueror, nor as a destroyer, but rather as a *Restorer* of the places and parts where it passeth; and although all its courses are extraordinarily quick and precipitate, yet they are so well measured and so well directed that no part of the body misseth them, and that none of its steps is unuseful, but rather very beneficial to all the places where it passeth."

"To judge well of the effects which this Volatile Salt [of Vipers?] can produce in our bodies, we must know its manner of operation, which is to open, to comminute, to attenuate, to pierce, and to drive to the extreme parts of the body, and through the pores of the skin, — [I must interpose the remark, that this is all said in a moral, and not a physical sense,] — all the impurities and all the strange [heterogene] bodies, that can get out by those ways. Further, it is an enemy to all corruption, very friendly and very agreeable to our nature, which it assists and fortifies, enabling it to expel, not only by the pores of the skin, but by siege, and by all the emunctories of the body, the superfluous humors which molest it; whence it comes to pass, that it produces admirable effects upon a thousand occasions, curing a great number of sicknesses, or at least giving great relief therein, even in those that are most refractory and most difficult to cure; such as apoplexies, lethargies, convulsions, agues, and many other maladies, believed to have their source in the *brain*."

If this writer had said that a purified conscience regulates many wanderings of the intellect, he would *openly* have said what he really meant, and what no one denies.

But I have yet many things to say, even at the hazard of being tedious, before I enter upon the proofs that Man is the central figure in Alchemy and Hermetic Philosophy, and that the conscience is the starting-point in pursuit of the Philosopher's Stone.

A consideration of perhaps more importance than all others is, that the conscience cannot be said in itself to err; in other words, the conscience cannot sin. It sits in judgment upon every man, approving the good and condemning the bad, but in itself it is incorruptible. The expression, a bad conscience, as when we say a man is troubled with a bad conscience, is not properly said of the conscience, but of the man whom a good conscience condemns.

I have no disposition to enter upon a metaphysical discussion, but, in order to explain the view I take of Alchemy, it is necessary for me to make apparent, if possible, that, in cases where many suppose that the conscience is in error, the error is not in the conscience, but in the judgment employed in applying means for the accomplishment of *ends*. In this way the most atrocious and abominable things have been done with the purest conscience, that is, the best intentions in the world. This admission may at first be thought equivalent to a complete surrender of the principle just assumed; but it is not so.

The conscience has reference to *ends*, and not to *means*, except where these are considered in themselves, and regarded as *ends*. Whether the sacrifice of Charles the First was well or ill done, is not a question for the conscience, but for the judgment, which is employed in determining whether that sacrifice was necessary to produce a certain *end*, the end only being the object of the conscience. A patriot loves his country, and endeavors to serve it, and this is universally esteemed a virtue; but in seeking the good of his country, he may mistake the *means* and plunge his country into irreparable evils. In this, and in every supposable case, the conscience decides upon the end, or, more clearly what I mean, the man is approved or condemned according to the end he aims at; and this is what all men have in view in passing moral judgments upon each other. We always seek to know the end a man aims at, in order to determine whether he is to be accepted or rejected in the court of conscience, and if the *end* is approved, a mistake in the means, however lamented, commands pity and not condemnation.

Now the end proposed in every case is a personal matter, about which no man, in his own case, can be mistaken;—if it is approved, the man is in a right condition for seeking means for effecting his end; but if the end be disapproved in the conscience, and the man still endeavors to attain it, it is manifest that the conscience is not in fault. This, by supposition, has executed its office and condemned the end, which, nevertheless, from other influences, the man is impelled to seek. A disruption now takes place. The unity is broken. The man has eaten of the forbidden fruit, and becomes an exile from Paradise. He is now a wanderer, and the question is, How is he to be recovered and brought back into the garden? The Alchemists, as I understand them, point with one voice to the conscience, as an uncorrupted and incorruptible virgin, which, though obscured by error, is the only *instrument* by which the wanderer can be recovered, with a preservation of what they call the "pondus," that is, the substantial reality of the individual.

The great "difficulty" is to bring the conscience into healthy action without *embasing* the subject, which the Alchemists say is always done when violence is used, all external influences and appliances, fears, etc., being called "corrosives." This is the doctrine of Alchemy; but it is wonderfully covered over and buried in figures and fables, for reasons which perhaps have less weight in this age than formerly.

In order still further to show the extent of the dominion of the conscience, I must refer to what men call *honor*, and observe that there is no *prin-*

ciple of honor in man except this one of the conscience. I, of course, mean true honor, and not a blind deference to a conventional code determined upon some arbitrarily conceived notions of narrow-minded, ignorant, arrogant, and domineering men, having only a local existence and influence. In a strict sense, nothing is honorable but what is right, and it *ought* to be very plain that nothing *wrong* can be honorable. The principle that determines what is right, determines also what is truly honorable; and therefore, whether we say it is right to live honorably, or honorable to live rightly, we say the same thing.

Most codes of honor, as they are called, are sustained by a love of reputation, by which men submit their conduct to the rule of some external law; but even here, the subjects of this law either approve the law, which may happen, or they persuade themselves that it is *right* to conform to the law prescribed by a given society in which they live; or, if not, they cannot feel satisfied with themselves while living in compliance with it.

I will add here, that the conscience is also the only principle of virtue; for virtue does not lie in a *judgment* of what may contribute to one's well-being in a prudential sense, except where virtue itself is recognized also as the highest prudence. Prudence may be a virtue, but virtue is not defined by prudence; somewhat as we may say that blue is a color, but color cannot be defined by saying it is blue.

I will even go further, and say that most, if not all, questions of religion are determined ultimately by an appeal to the same principle, the conscience. It is thus that men reason about the *duty* of attendance upon divine service, and of living in conformity with most of the customs of religious people.

The highest of all religious *duties* is that of obedience to God; and yet this, by the phraseology used to express it, has its sanction in the conscience. It is said to be *right* for the creature to obey the Creator. An obedience rendered upon any other ground would not be free, and when produced by either hope of reward or fear of punishment is destitute of virtue. A sense of duty made cheerful by love, is the true ground of that perfect obedience to God, which it is the object of all pure religion to secure.

There is nothing so offensive in the Koran as the continual denunciation of "hell-fire" against unbelievers, simply because, in the nature of the case, fear never yet made or can make an honest man.

To determine what particular conduct is acceptable to God may be the office of other principles, in which men may differ very widely. But this is a difference of judgment applied to matters of fact, in settling questions of history, etc.; but whenever it can be decided that any particular conduct in man is pleasing to God, the *duty* of compliance is already prescribed in the conscience.

In addition to all I have said, there is one mode of stating the question which would seem to exclude all controversy; for let it be supposed that some other law besides that of the conscience is of greater authority, how can it be authenticated but by the conscience itself, which must ultimately be appealed to for a sanction of the law? for to say that a man *ought* to be governed by any law whatever, is to use the language of the conscience. If any rule can therefore be proposed before the conscience which of *right* demands obedience, it would then be *wrong* to obey the law of conscience; but to do right is the very essence of the law of conscience; so that, in preferring another law, a man is reduced to the absurdity of affirming that it is wrong to do right.

There is no place where the power of the conscience is so fully manifested as at the confessional, and there are no people in the world more capable of understanding the force of the conscience than the Catholic priesthood. No doubt many principles operate collaterally in the practice of confession, especially the passions of hope and fear; but in a vast majority of cases conscience is the chief working power that supports the confessional, and in some sense may be thought the support of the whole fabric of the Catholic Church.

In most cases, the word *spirit* in the Psalms and Proverbs, as well as elsewhere in Scripture, means *conscience;* as in Prov. xviii. 14, — "The spirit of a man will sustain his infirmity; but a wounded spirit who can bear?" — which means just this, that a good conscience will sustain a man under infirmities, but no man can bear a wounded conscience; and because this is the case, and because the means of *reconciliation* are not so much the object of conscience as of judgment, which is liable to err, multitudes of men seek it in the *forms* of an established creed adjudged by others to be solely efficacious. The confessional affords the *means* of a reconciliation with God, that is, with one's own conscience; for it comes to this at last. No Catholic can feel that he is accepted with God until he has satisfied his own conscience by a compliance with what is judged to be necessary for that purpose. All sacrifices, modes of worship, compliance with church forms and ceremonies, etc., have at last but the one great object, to wit, a feeling of oneness or acceptance with God, and this in its essence means just this and no more, that a man may become reconciled in his own conscience. Leave but the slightest flaw upon the conscience, and man to this extent is an outlaw and an exile from God's presence; and this is not a contingent, but a necessary result.

The difficulty in this question does not lie in the conscience, but, as I have already said, in the judgment as to means employed in executing the dictates of conscience. For example, it is right for a man to seek the glory of God; but to do this intelligently requires the most profound of all knowledge, the knowledge of God, and of what is for his glory: or, if it be right for a man to seek beatitude either here or hereafter, a similar species of knowledge is required. Whether this knowledge is possible except to a purified conscience may be a question, and on this point the Alchemists might have to defend themselves; I merely suggest the point, to show that it has occurred to me.

If any one should now ask what this conscience is, and what its origin, I would put him upon his conscience to answer, quite sure that, if he has one, he need but interrogate it; while, if he has no conscience, it is certain he will never be brought to the bar of it; but it is equally certain that such a man will never know what it is to be free, but he must live and die a slave to his passions, and shall never know true peace of mind.

I do not wish to be understood as saying that *mercury, our mercury, philosophical mercury,* etc. are expressions used always in one sense. Very far from it. Mercury is often used for man simply, but sometimes it is used for nature in a universal sense; then for what some understand by the spirit of nature, and again for the spirit of man, every writer taking some latitude in the use of this, and indeed of every other word used symbolically, purposely, it would seem, to compel the student to verify what is said by testing it with "the possibility of nature." Some of the writers invent new words altogether, having no meaning at all, leaving the reader to divine the meaning by the qualities attributed to it; as if one should describe *erif*, by saying that it is something by which an apple might be roasted, it would not be difficult to discover that *erif* meant *fire*.

As a general rule, the conscience is called philosophical mercury, or our mercury; but, by whatever name it may be called, it is the *instrument* of improvement, and the *way to the end.*

I admit that the work is "circular," as the writers say themselves, and that the end is in some sense the beginning also, which perhaps, as one single point, *is the greatest secret of the whole matter.* Hence the writers tell us that, to make gold, we must have gold; which is not very obscure, after all, if we understand that whoever would find truth must *be* true: and this is Scriptural also, for whoever would find grace must have grace to seek it.

We are in the midst of the universe, and know nothing either of its beginning or ending, except as both are contained in the present; and how to understand this cannot but be difficult, and must reduce all reasoning upon the subject to a circle or a nullity. But the fact precedes all argument, and so does the conscience, and both equally prostrate all attempts to ignore them.

Having spoken of various uses of the word *mer-*

cury, I may as well say, that, in a great multitude of places, some two words will be found coupled together, yet not always in the same sense; as, Sol and Luna, gold and silver, masculine and feminine, brother and sister, the Doves of Diana, *circulatum majus* and *circulatum minus*, the greater magnet and the lesser magnet; and, indeed, an endless variety of other names, the sense of which must be determined by the context, tested by "the possibility of nature." It may surprise a novice in such studies to observe the innumerable quantity of *correlates* to be found in nature, beginning with the macrocosm and microcosm; for we have cause and effect, active and passive, heaven and earth, divine and human, upper and lower, good and evil, hope and fear, soul and body, and an endless quantity of other doubles; for we read, " All things are double one against another; and God hath made nothing imperfect. One thing establishes the good of another." (Ecclesiasticus xlii. 24.) Where I have ventured to use the words *Soul and Body*, in the interpretation of some of these doubles, I must be excused for begging the reader not to imagine that by the bare use of these words the things are known; and before he thinks he knows these things, I would recommend him to look for them in the "chest" where Wilhelm Meister found David and Goliath peaceably side by side.

The reader will observe that I am merely endeavoring to suggest the mode of writing adopted by the Alchemists, without defending it. I intend to show presently that the conscience, a complete knowledge of which must not be assumed, is the touchstone of all their writings, and that *the way* to the Philosopher's Stone is through or by means of it. Nothing can exceed the simplicity of it from this point of view, while from another point of view there is no mystery exceeding it, for it is commensurate with life itself. It is the mystery of life.

If the conscience is the way to the Philosopher's Stone, I hear exclaimed, why not speak out plainly about it? what is the need of this mystical talk about salt, sulphur, and mercury? This question, no doubt, often recurs. I have already stated what I consider two reasons for the secret mode of writing, and may add here, that the very simplicity of the doctrine, or the entrance to it, provokes a doubt or denial of the efficacy of this sort of mercury in working any very extraordinarily good end; hence men look abroad, away from themselves, and would have some marvellous, if not miraculous and incomprehensible, means of bringing about the hope of better things in some distant future. Besides, almost all men wish to be saved in or with their sins ("superfluities"), and not by a separation from them. The doctrine of Christ, which the Alchemists strictly follow, is unmistakably against this; still, with multitudes of men the hope of the future is but little better than an artificial compromise, by which the sinner *consents* to accept the promise of a future upon condition, secretly stipulated, of being undisturbed in the present. To be sure, the future has its claims upon us; but perhaps the only way to secure it is to be right now, and keep so.

As the word *mercury* is used in several senses, so is that of *fire*. In some cases it means the intellect, but in general it means the conscience in the individual: sometimes it means what is not inappropriately called the public conscience: or it is the *principle* in the *race*, which is perpetual, surviving all fluctuations in society and governments; it lives on in defiance of all sophistry, and remains for ever undisturbed by philosophical and religious disputes.

Bishop Taylor has said, that " God hath given

us conscience to be in his stead to us, to give us laws, and to exact obedience to those laws, to punish them that prevaricate, and to reward the obedient. And therefore," continues this great man, " conscience is called the household guardian and domestic god, the spirit or angel of the place; and when we call God to witness, we only mean that our conscience is right, and that God, and God's vicar, our conscience, knows it."

" Conscience," says Dr. South, " is a Latin word, though with an English termination, and, according to the very notation of it, imports a double or joint knowledge; to wit, one of a divine law or rule, and the other of a man's own action; and so is properly the application of a general law to a particular instance of practice."

But the conscience, as I have repeatedly said, is only *the way* or *means* in what is called the *great work*; indispensable, indeed; for without it the Alchemists say that nothing can be done in the " Art"; but this initial point being secured, they then speak of *sowing*, in this *philosophical mercury*, what they call the PHILOSOPHICAL GOLD, which is sometimes called Venus.

This is Love; the love of God and man; about which I confess I am unwilling to say much, lest

I venture beyond my depth. Those who wish to see some account of it in Plato may consult the Banquet, and learn to substitute for the vulgar notion of Platonic Love, an inspiration of the love of Truth; for this is the Platonic Love, engrafted only on a purified conscience, and inaccessible to a profane man while living in his sins.

For the proofs now of what I have thus far advanced, I shall cite passages from several authors referred to by both the French writer and the Reviewer, and from some not mentioned by either. They both refer to *Isaac Hollandus*, (of the fifteenth century, according to Du Fresnoy,) but give no account of either him or his work.

I will make a few extracts from his writings, which will be easily understood with the explanations I have given. The title of the volume is: "A Work of Saturn. By John Isaac Hollandus. Published in English, 1670."

I have said that the Alchemists often speak of man by the names of metals, and that they frequently call these by astronomical names. In this treatise, *Saturn* stands for *Lead;* but as by Lead is meant man, as will be seen presently, the real title of the work is *A Treatise of Man.* To guard against misapprehension, even on a minor point, I should say, that by *Saturn* is sometimes meant, not merely man, but man in a state of *humility*.

The Preface by the English translator, being short and "suggestive," I will copy entire, as follows.

"*Courteous Reader*, — The philosophers have written much of their *Lead*, which is prepared out of *Antimony*, as Basilius hath taught; and I am of opinion that this *Saturnine* work of the most excellent philosopher, M. John Isaac Hollandus, is not to be understood of common lead, if the matter of the stone be not much more thereby intended, but of the *Philosopher's Lead*. But whether the vulgar Saturn be the matter of the philosopher's stone or not, you will receive sufficient satisfaction from the following work, which is published for the benefit of all the *lovers of this Art*, because it expounds and declares the Stone of Fire. *Vale.*"

The Stone of Fire is *the end* of the *practice*, of which I do not wish to speak at large. I only insist that the subject is man, and I shall endeavor to point out *the way*, — to wit, by the conscience.

" In the name of the Lord. Amen.

" My child must know that the stone, called the Philosopher's Stone, comes out of Saturn.

" And know, my child, for a truth, that in the

whole vegetable world there is no higher nor greater secret than there is in Saturn: [that is, man is the miracle of the universe, and contains within himself the greatest of secrets, — which those ought to believe who regard him as the image of God:] for we do not find that perfection in gold which is found in Saturn; because, internally, it is good gold [it contains the image of God]; herein all of the philosophers are agreed; and it wants nothing else but that first you remove what is *superfluous* in it; and then, that you turn its inside outwards, which is its redness: then it will be good gold. [This is only another way of teaching with that of Isaiah. I do not say it is as good a method, but I affirm that Hollandus means the same as Isaiah, where he says (chap. i.): "Wash you, make you clean; put away the evil of your doings from before mine eyes," &c. Verse 22 of this chapter is in the language appropriated by the Alchemists: "Thy silver is become dross, thy *wine* mixed with water."] For," says Hollandus, in continuation, "gold cannot be made so easily from anything as from Saturn; for Saturn is easily dissolved and congealed, and its *mercury* may be more easily extracted from it. [The theory here is, that the conscience will manifest itself and become active, when the *superfluities* in which it lies buried are removed; in, perhaps, the sense of James i. 21.] And this mercury extracted from Saturn, being purified and sublimed, as mercury is usually sublimed, I tell thee, my child, that the same mercury is as good as the mercury extracted out of gold in all operations."

An allusion is here intended, that all men are of one nature essentially, and that all partake of the image of the Eternal.

"If Saturn be gold internally, as in truth it is, then must its mercury be as good as the mercury of gold.

"My child, lock this up in thy heart and understanding: this Saturn is the stone, which the philosopher's will not name; its name has been concealed unto this day. . . . . . The name remains concealed, because of the evils which might proceed from its being known. [Observe the reasons already given for secrecy, especially the second reason, *viz.* the danger of proposing a change in the *ground* of duty, from that of a hope of reward, to a sense of duty, *as it is a duty*, independently of both hope and fear.]

"All of the strange parables which the philosophers have spoken mystically of a stone, a moon, a furnace, a vessel, — all this is Saturn [that is, all is said of man]; for you must not put any strange thing [anything foreign to its nature], but only that which comes out of it. There is none so poor in this world, that cannot operate and promote this work; for *Luna* may be easily made of Saturn, in a short time, [here *Luna* stands for the affections purified,] and in a little time longer *Sol* may be made from it. [By *Sol*, here, I understand the intellect, which becomes clarified in proportion as the affections become purified; a great deal of what is called intellect — a brisk smartness and cunning cleverness, the product of animal spirits aided by a good memory — is not the true *Sol*.]

"And though a man be poor, yet may he very well attain unto it, and may be employed in making the philosopher's stone."

That is, every man, no matter how humble his vocation, *may do the best he can*, in his place, — may "love mercy, do justly, and walk humbly with God"; and what more doth God require of any man? (Micah vi. 8.) M. Figuier observes, that a great number of authors certify that the poor possess the philosopher's stone, as well as the rich; and certainly they do, if we understand by it truth, goodness, moral perfection, the Divine blessing.

Sandivogius says: "I doubt not but many men of good consciences and affections do secretly enjoy this gift of God." Yet this could not open the eyes of M. Figuier.

"Wherefore, my child," continues Hollandus, "all that we have need of is concealed in Saturn; for in it is a perfect mercury; in it are all the colors of the world."

That is, the whole universe in some sense lies in the nature of man, whence have proceeded all religions, all philosophies, all histories, all fables, all poesy, all arts and sciences.

"The eye of man cannot endure anything that is imperfect, how little soever it be; though it should be the least atom of dust, it would cause pain, so that he could not rest. But if you take the quantity of a bean of Saturn, shave it smooth and round, and put it into the eye, it will cause no pain at all."

This is only a mode of saying that the conscience, the eye of the soul, cannot bear the least falsehood; but it receives truth as congenerous with its nature.

"The reason is, that Saturn is internally perfect, even as gold and precious stones. By these and other speeches, [dark sayings, Prov. i. 6,] you may observe that Saturn is our philosopher's stone, and our Latten, out of which our mercury and our stone is extracted with small labor, little art and expense, and in a short time.

"Wherefore I admonish you, my child, and all those who know its name, that you conceal it from the people, [that is, from people in general, who have neither leisure nor inclination to think of these things,] by reason of the evil that might otherwise arise; *and you shall call the stone our Latten; and call the vinegar, water,* wherein our stone is to be washed."

The vinegar is the conscience, wherein the man is to be washed. It is called by infinite other names, as oil, honey, wormwood, &c., &c.

"This is the stone and the water whereof the philosophers have written so many volumes.

"This stone is the true *aurum potabile*, the true quintessence which we seek; and we seek no other thing in the world but this stone. Therefore the philosophers say, that whoever knows our stone, and can prepare it, [that is, perfect it,] needs no more; wherefore they sought this thing, and no other."

In short, it is the one thing needful, or the way to it, to wit, the perfect approval of a conscience purified in the presence of God; for, examine the matter as closely as we may, we shall find no ground for supposing God's approval of us but our own self-approval, ascertained in the closet and not put to vote in the market-place.

Thus writes Isaac Hollandus, who, M. Figuier and the English Reviewer imagine, was in pursuit of an agent for the transmutation of metals.

Another of the genuine Alchemists, referred to by the Reviewer, is Artephius, (of the twelfth century, according to Du Fresnoy,) whom he laughs at for saying that he had lived a thousand years. He is not the first to ridicule this, Swift and Butler having fully occupied the ground. As old a writer as Sallust, the Platonic philosopher, in his treatise on the Gods, has given a rule for the interpretation of extravagances, and even abominations, found in old poems and philosophies. That, says he, which in a literal sense is manifestly absurd and impossible, must be understood in some other sense.

It was upon this principle that Philo interpreted the sacred writings of his nation, and Origen pursued the same method with the New Testament.

In the case of Artephius, a slight acquaintance with the books of the Alchemists will inform any one that these writers, at times, call months *years*, weeks *months*, &c. Roger Bacon in one place speaks of a philosophic month, which he says is forty days. This may be ridiculous, but if any one is disposed to comment upon it, the whole should be taken together.

By this it appears that Artephius was something over eighty years of age when he wrote a work, as I say, upon *Man*, though the book purports to be on *Antimony*, which he defines as "a mineral participating of *Saturnine* parts [in the sense of Hollandus, who wrote of *Saturn*], and has in all respects the nature thereof."

That which Artephius calls *antimonial vinegar* is what Hollandus charged his pupil to call *water* (to "deceive the profane"). In plain words, as simple as it may seem, they both mean the conscience; and when Artephius says, that "without antimonial vinegar no metal can be *whitened*," he means, that without the conscience no man can be purified. Artephius calls it by many names, besides antimonial vinegar; as *acrid vinegar; oil; dissolving water; the fountain; balneum maniæ; the preternatural fire; the secret, hidden, and invisible fire; pure, clear water;* and many other names; and says that "it is the only apt and natural medium, by which we ought to resolve [dissolve, *humiliate*] the perfect bodies of *Sol* and *Luna* [Soul and Body], by a wonderful and solemn dissolution, with a *preservation* of the species, and without any destruction, unless it be to a new, more noble, and better form of generation; *to wit*, into the perfect philosopher's stone."

"Now this *water*," says he, "is a certain middle substance, clear as fine silver, which ought to receive the Tinctures [the essences] of *Sol* and *Luna* [Soul and Body], so that they may be congealed and changed into a white [pure] and *living* earth."

By the use of the expression *middle substance*, Artephius would have us think of the *conscience* as something between the Soul and Body, without being precisely either, and yet the tie of both, the Soul being the fabricating cause of the Body, and the Body being the embodiment of the Soul, — as Swedenborg expresses it. But whoever would study the conscience must not be deluded by mere words.

"This water," says Artephius, "needs the perfect bodies, that with them after the dissolution it may be congealed, fixed, and coagulated into a white earth."

If the reader will weigh distinctly each passage, thinking of the *nature of the thing*, and not be over-critical upon the manner of expressing it, he may with no great difficulty understand the *theory* of these writers. The truth or falsehood of the theory, is an independent inquiry, about which, of course, there may be differences of opinion. The first step is dissolution (sometimes called calcination, and by many other names), effected by the conscience as a spiritual power, by which *the man* is summoned, as it were, into the presence of God, and feels the nothingness of all mere human attractions, and the impossibility of evasion, prevarication, and deceit, and thus becomes as a little child, according to the requirement of Mark x. 15, the instant of submission being also the beginning of a new life.

"But their solution," continues Artephius, "is also their coagulation: they have one and the same operation, for one is not dissolved, but the other is congealed. Nor is there any other *water* which can dissolve the bodies, but that which *abideth with them in matter and form.*"

I must call attention to the principle just indicated, as containing a fund of wisdom for all who are charged with the moral and spiritual education of man, who is not "effectually" improved but by the action of something proper to his nature, and which remains with it. This is what Hollandus means, when he says of *Saturn*, that nothing must be put into it but that which arises from it. Artephius proceeds: —

" It cannot be *permanent* unless it be of the nature of the other bodies, that they may be made *one*. Thus you see that nature is to be amended by its own like nature; that is, gold and silver [he means *Sol* and *Luna*] are to be exalted in our *water* [the water of Hollandus], as our water also with those bodies; which water is called the medium of the soul, *without which nothing can be done in our art*. It is a vegetable, mineral, and animal fire, which conserves the fixed spirits [the essence or substance] of *Sol* and *Luna*, but destroys and conquers their bodies; for it destroys, overturns, and changes bodies and metallic forms [that is, Sol and Luna, modally considered], making them to be no bodies but a fixed spirit."

Artephius then urges, altogether in figures however, that the *water* cannot penetrate imperfect metals in their *dry, hard state*, and therefore they must be *softened* and brought into a "fluid matter" (of course, this is all metaphorical); but this is effected by the *water* itself, which " attenuates, alters, and softens the bodies, to wit, *Sol* and *Luna*, that so they may be mixed with other bodies." The reader may remember the properties attributed to the volatile salt of vipers, and may understand that a common idea prevails. Artephius now speaks of it under another name, and says:—

"It is an oil by nature hot, subtle, penetrating, sinking through and entering into other bodies: it is called the perfect or great Elixir, and the hidden secret of the wise searchers of nature. He, therefore, who knows this salt of *Sol* and *Luna*, and its generation and preparation, and afterwards how to commix it, and make it *homogene* with other imperfect bodies, knows, in truth, one of the greatest secrets of nature, and the only way that leads to perfection."

"These Bodies," he continues, "thus dissolved by our water, [that is, the Soul and Body dissolved by the conscience, and not brought into a state of humiliation by mortified pride, for this "color" effects nothing in the art,] are called *Argent vive*, which is not without its sulphur, nor the sulphur without the fixedness of *Sol* and *Luna;* because gold and silver [*Sol* and *Luna*] are the particular means or medium in the form through which nature passes in the perfecting and completing thereof. And this *Argent vive* is called our esteemed and valuable salt, being animated and pregnant; and our *Fire*, because it is nothing but Fire: yet not fire, but sulphur; and not sulphur only, but also *quicksilver*, drawn from *Sol* and *Luna* by our *water*, and reduced into a Stone of great price: that is to say, it is the matter or substance of *Sol* and *Luna*, or *silver* and *gold* altered from vileness to nobility."

Artephius calls it a "living water which comes to moisten the earth, that it may spring forth, and in due season bring forth much fruit"; comparing it to rain, saying, "it penetrates the bodies and makes one new body of two bodies."

"This *aqua vitæ*, or water of Life [here are other names for the same thing], being rightly ordered [i. e. rightly or *naturally* brought into action], and disposed with the body, it whitens it, and converts or changes it into a white color [purifies it]."

Artephius then calls it *Azoth*, and the *water washing* Latten. The reader will remember that Hollandus called his Saturn *Latten*, and his vinegar *water*.

The philosopher now exclaims: "How precious, then, and how great a thing, is this water! for without it *the work* could never be done or perfected: it is also called *vas naturæ*, the belly, the womb, the receptacle of the tincture, the earth, the nurse. It is the royal fountain in which the King and Queen [*Sol* and *Luna* again, for the names are infinitely varied] bathe themselves; and the mother which must be put into and sealed up within the belly of her infant; and that is Sol himself, who proceeded from her, and whom she brought forth; and therefore they have loved one another as mother and son, and are conjoined together, because they came from one root and are of the same substance and nature. And because this water is the water of the vegetable life, it causes the dead body to vegetate, increase, and spring forth, and *to rise from death to life*, by being dissolved first and then sublimed. And in doing this the body is converted into a spirit, and the spirit afterwards into a body; and then is made the amity, the peace, the concord, and the *union* of the contraries, to wit, between the body and the spirit, which reciprocally or naturally change their natures, which they receive and communicate one to another through their most minute parts."

He goes on to say that "in this operation the Body is made a Spirit, of a most subtle nature; and again, the Spirit is corporified and changed into the nature of the Body, with the Bodies, whereby our Stone" [can any one doubt the meaning of the author? that, *man*] "consists of *a Body, a Soul, and a Spirit.*"

"It appears, then," says Artephius, "that this composition *is not a work of the hands*, but a change of the natures; because nature dissolves, and joins itself, sublimes and lifts itself up, and grows white, being separated from the *fæces* [i. e. superfluities, as Hollandus called them]...... Our Brass or Latten then is to be made to ascend by the degrees of Fire, *but of its own accord, freely, and without violence.* But when it ascends on high, it is born in the Air or Spirit, and is changed into a spirit; and becomes *Life with Life.* And by such an operation it is that the Body is made of a subtle nature, and the Spirit is incorporated with the Body, *and made one with it;* and by such a sublimation, conjunction, and raising up, the whole, Body and Spirit, are made white [pure]."

Nearly all of the writers quote a saying attributed to "old Osthanes," — that *Nature se joint par nature; nature s'éjouet en nature; nature amende nature; nature aime nature; nature surmonte nature; nature perfectionne nature; nature contient nature et nature est contenue par nature;* and several of them caution their readers to keep these principles strongly in mind.

All of the writers agree that "violence" is not to be used. They designate all appliances to force man into goodness as "corrosives," "*aqua fortis,*" &c., and say that where they are used, they can only produce a *surface tincture;* they always "embase the metal," and make it unfit for the artist.

It seems impossible not to perceive that Artephius is writing of *Man*, and is endeavoring to indicate some process by which man may be said to pass, under the discipline of God and Nature, from a chaotic state of ignorance and passion to a certain *unity*.

"The Spirit," says he, "penetrates, the Body fixes, and the Soul joins together, tinges, and whitens. From these three united together is our Stone made; to wit, Sol, Luna, and Mercury. Therefore, with this our *golden-water*, a natural substance is extracted, exceeding all natural substances; and so, except the bodies be broken and destroyed, imbibed and made subtle and fine, thriftily and diligently managed, till they are abstracted from or lose their grossness or solid substance, and be changed into a thin and subtle spirit, all our labor will be in vain. And unless the bodies be made no bodies, or incorporeal, that is, be converted into the philosopher's mercury, *there is no rule of Art yet found out to work by.*"

"Now this operation or work," says Artephius, "is a thing of no great labor to him that knows and understands it; nor is the matter so dear, considering how small a quantity doth suffice, that it should cause any man to withdraw his hand from it. It is indeed a work so short and easy, that it may well be called a woman's work and the play of children. Go to, then, my son, put up thy supplications to God Almighty; be diligent in searching the books of the learned in this science; for one book openeth another; think and meditate of these things profoundly; and avoid all things that vanish in, or will not endure, the fire [avoid everything that wounds the conscience], because from those adustible, perishing, or consuming things, you can never attain to the perfect matter, which is only found in the digesting of your water extracted from Sol and Luna."

"This water is the true tincture, separated from all its black fæces; and our Brass or Latten is prepared with our Water, purified and brought to a white color."

"Which white color is not obtained but by decoction, and coagulation of the water. Decoct therefore continually; *wash away the blackness from the Latten, not with your hands, but with the Stone, or the Fire, or our second mercurial water, which is the true Tincture.*"

"This separation of the pure from the impure is not done with hands; but Nature herself does it, and brings it to perfection by a *circular* operation."

"Wherefore decoct the Body in our white water, viz. *Mercury*, till it be dissolved into blackness [humility], and then by a continual decoction let it be deprived of the same blackness, and the body so dissolved will at length ascend or rise with a white [pure] soul."

It may be needless, perhaps, to turn the attention of the reader to the "circular" nature of this operation, for he can hardly fail to see that *the water extracts the water, which extracts the water;* and, as I have already intimated, perhaps the most difficult of all the secrets in Hermetic Philosophy lies precisely here. If the reader desires to understand anything of this philosophy, I would recommend him to throw aside, for the moment, everything like a captious disposition, and, avoiding hypercriticism, reflect upon the course of nature, and see how impossible it is, by what the Germans call the understanding, "judging according to sense," to seize upon a first or a last, or a first which is not also a last; and after first losing himself in this maze, he may find himself all the stronger.

After turning this difficult point, he may be in

a good condition for understanding the wonderful text, "Whosoever will save his life shall lose it; and whosoever will lose his life for my sake, shall find it."

I must not omit to say, that thus far Artephius is chiefly speaking of what some of the writers call the "base" of the work, and although I have just hinted at the *end*, I do not propose to speak of it at length. This can only be known by those who put into requisition *the means;* for nature never does anything but *by means*, and according to them. Every man must reap as he sows.

The *Secret Book of Artephius* contains some twenty chapters or more, in the course of which what is called the "great work," and sometimes the "Divine work," is indicated by many repetitions, in different ways. The author points out more of what may be called the theory of the Unity in Trinity (or Trinity in Unity), than is usually met with in these peculiar books.

Basil Valentine (born 1414), another Alchemist referred to by the Reviewer, also indicates the Unity, writing as Artephius did of Antimony; that is, of man under this name. Everything these authors say is obscure until the reader *takes the idea;* for example: "Now," says Basilius, "let the reader consider, and observe it as a thing worthy of note, that the true *Unicorn's-horn*, sophisticated by no fallacy, repels all venom from itself; nor can it assume or draw to itself anything of venom, as is manifest by experience."

Can any one read such a passage, and imagine that the author intended to be understood literally? Who has ever known such an animal as the Unicorn? Precisely because this *one*-horned animal is fabulous, it answered the purpose of Basil, which was to teach that the absolute Unity is necessarily free from all evil, and incapable of being affected by it. But what has this to do with Antimony? It has much to do with it, if, under the name of Antimony, Basil's subject was Man.

Basil Valentine wrote of man under a great variety of symbols, but his principal work is that entitled *The Triumphal Chariot of Antimony.* A few passages will show that he held opinions in common with all the Alchemists.

"Consider," says he, "and observe these things diligently; for this principal key is of great concern: *Antimony, which contains in itself its own vinegar,* ought to be so prepared that all its *venenosity* may be taken away. He who then useth it, conceives no venom thereby, but rather drives away and casts out all poison from himself."

Basilius is treating of man, in whom, as an instrument of purification, there is contained its own vinegar, that is, the "water" of Hollandus, by the use of which man may expel and cast out of himself all sin. He proceeds:—

"Therefore, in the preparation of Antimony consists the Key of Alchemy, by which it is dissolved, divided, and separated; as in calcination, reverberation, sublimation, etc.; also in extracting its essence, and in *vivifying its mercury*, which mercury must afterwards be precipitated in a fixed powder: likewise, by Art and a due method, of it may be made an *oil* for the cure of diseases."

In another place he says: "You are to know, that in Antimony there is *a Spirit* which affects whatsoever is in it, or can proceed from it, in an *invisible way* and manner; no otherwise than as in the magnet is absconded a certain *invisible power*, as we shall more largely treat in its own place, where we speak of the magnet."

Perhaps I ought to say, that many of these writers speak of man as a *Magnet*, having in itself a principle by which it seeks the great Magnet, and will never rest until it "lies level with it."

To show that his subject is the same as that of those who wrote of *Saturn* or *Lead*, Basil says:

"But that we may also say something of the *Lead* of the philosophers, let the curious searchers of nature know, that between *Antimony* and common *Lead* there is a certain near affinity, and they hold a strict friendship, the one with the other."

He concludes a work on the *Magnet* in the following manner, as if he would compel the commonest dullard to divine his meaning.

"Allegorical expressions betwixt the Holy Trinity and the Philosopher's Stone.

"Dear Christian Lover, and well-wisher to the Blessed Art: how graciously and miraculously hath the Holy Trinity created the Philosopher's Stone. For God the Father is a Spirit, and yet maketh himself known under the notion of a Man, as where he speaketh, *Gen.* chap. i., Let us make man after our own image: again, the expressions where he speaketh of his mouth, eyes, hands, and feet: so the philosopher's mercury is held to be a *spiritual Body*, as philosophers call him. God the Father begetteth his only Son Jesus Christ, which is God and man, and is without sin, neither needed he to die; but he laid down his life freely, and rose again, for his brethren and sisters' sake, that they might live with him eternally without sin. So is *Sol*, or *Gold*, without defect, and if fixed, holds out gloriously in all fiery examens; but by reason of its imperfect and sick brethren and sisters [the Soul and Body are often called male and female, brother and sister], it dieth and riseth gloriously, redeemeth and tingeth them unto eternal Life, making them perfect unto good gold.

" The third person of the Trinity is God the Holy Ghost, a comforter sent by our Lord *Christ Jesus* unto his believing Christians, who strengtheneth and comforteth them in faith, unto Eternal Life: even so is the spirit of material *Sol*, or of the *Body of Mercury*, when they come together. These are two spirits, God the Father and God the Holy Ghost. But God the Son, a glorified man, is even as our glorified and fixed *Sol*, or Philosopher's Stone; since *Lapis* is called *Trinus*, namely, out of two waters [*Sol* and *Luna* considered essentially] or spirits of mineral and of vegetable; and of the animal of sulphur of Sol. These are the *Two* and *Three*, and yet but *One:* if you understand it not, then you are not likely to succeed. Thus by way of *similitude* I have delineated unto thee sufficiently the *Universal*. Pray to God for a blessing, for without Him you are not likely to prosper at all."

It seems amazing, in view of such passages, that the real subject and object of Alchemy should have escaped the observation of almost every one except those who cultivated the study; in so much, that there is scarcely a fragment of general literature in allusion to the Alchemists but what implies that they were in pursuit of gold, when, except some "deluded, sottish ignorants," nothing can be more certain than that their purpose was wholly religious.

The reader can hardly fail to see the *theory* indicated by Basilius, right or wrong: and that he considered *man* as consisting (not *composed*, in a mechanical sense) of Body, Soul, and Spirit; that the latter appears in the form of conscience, itself sinless and incapable of sin, though associated with a "sick" brother and sister, for whose sake it mystically dies, but only to work out a purification, when the same spirit is regarded as a Magnet, or as possessing a magnetic virtue (call it Love) by which it seeks the universal Magnet, in which alone it has its Life and finds its eternal resting-place.

But see how one of these writers preludes in a somewhat antiquated language on this subject:—

"Well did the primitive Grecian give the name Αλήθεια unto TRUTH: whose consanguinity, nay, consubstantiality of essence with the Human Soul, which the divine philosophy of Moses hath defined to be the *breath of God*, doth exactly make out that Etymology. For so incessant a *magnetism*, or congenerous Love, doth the Soul hold unto *Truth*, that she can know no real or permanent satisfaction, in the fruition of any other object; but like the Aguish magnetified needle, reels to and fro, in a phrenzy of inquietude, distracted twixt various apparitions, until she lie parallel unto the centre, or *unity* thereof; but having once fixed [the reader should note this expression, for it points to what the Alchemists call the "fixation" of the matter of the Stone] in that happy position, she is, by an eternal *union*, identified or assimilated unto that twin of herself, and in that mysterious penetration of Homogenial forms meets her Beatitude, which can never know defect of satiety, alterity of desires, or remission of intensity."

The Reviewer thinks Basil Valentine, in seeking for the "Mercurius Philosophorum" in Antimony, though he missed what he sought, discovered a "valuable spirit of Salt, what we call the hydrochloric acid."

The reader is now prepared to judge whether the *Spirit* sought for by Basilius in Antimony had any affinity with *hydrochloric acid!*

I know very well, however, that he did not lose sight of the actual mineral, following in this respect the example of all symbolic writers, who work up as much double truth as possible, without prejudice to the real object under the veil.

Webster, in a volume entitled *Metallographia* (1671), has written a Treatise of actual metals; but he has concluded every chapter Alchemically (or Hermetically) by writing, under a mask, of man. A hasty reader would only be mystified a little, but any one acquainted with the mode of writing adopted by the Alchemists would easily detect the disciple of Hermes.

Van Suchten, like Basil Valentine and Artephius, wrote of Antimony, 1670; but his subject is also man, and his principles coincide entirely with those already cited. He opens his work in these words: —

"It is not our purpose to write and dispute, out of what *Antimony* first cometh, as some have done."

That is, the author will not undertake the (vain) inquiry into the origin of man, but he will take him as he finds him. This is what he means in this opening passage of his work.

He soon declares that, " in matter [substance], metals and antimony are all one," and discloses the Alchemist by saying that " Antimony is an imperfect metal, and in philosophy is called *Saturn* [the Saturn of Hollandus], of which Rhasis writeth, saying, that in Saturn, *Sol and Luna* [in the sense of active and passive] are contained in potentia, not visibly. Also Pythagoras saith, *all secrets are in Saturn;* and this Saturn is our Lead, which we physicians [philosophers] must know and understand; for it is created for us; it is *ours* and not another's. . . . . . Out of Antimony by Art is *aurum potabile* made. . . . . . This Art is named *Alchemy*. . . . . .

" Now for the *preparation* of Antimony, know that Antimony is an Earth wherein lieth a metal called *Mercury* [the mercury or water of Hollandus again]. This must the physician *draw from Antimony;* but the *miner* shall first melt Antimony from his mineral earth, wherein it grew, *and purify it*. . . . . . Thus is Mercury made out of Antimony, out of Saturn, Argent Vive, which belongeth to the physician; out of which he shall farther make *Luna*, and out of *Luna, Sol;* so hath his work an end."

Let any one compare this with the extract from Hollandus, and it will be seen that what one says of *Lead*, the other says of *Antimony;* but Lead is not Antimony, while nevertheless both of them may symbolize man, as they certainly do in the Hermetic writings under examination.

The second chapter of Van Suchten is, " of the venom of the physical mercury, his heat and sulphur, and of the glass of antimony," in which a second step is taken. By *glass* we are to understand purity, often spoken of as crystalline glass. It is the *White Earth* of Artephius.

The third chapter is much more abstruse, in which the author speaks of a certain Fire which is called, he says, *Donum Dei*, and proceeds: " The Alchemists — I understand not here," says he, " those sots who promise riches to others, yet are themselves beggars — have called this mystery the *Philosopher's Stone*, the *Blessed Holy Stone*, for this reason, that God hath placed it in an earthy, stony, and contemptible matter [man]. The Arabians have called it *Alchemy*, because Alchemy is an instrument which divideth the good from the bad; and what is not mature it matureth. The astronomers say it is Sol, that bringeth all things to maturity. So is this mystery, according to the *similitude*, called the Sun also. Paracelsus, in many places, calleth it Gold; as in that place where he saith, *Let gold be the seed, be thou the growing plant.*"

Here is a passage in condemnation of false Alchemists : —

" If thou dost object," says Van Suchten, " that not only common people, but also great nobles, have labored a long time in Alchemy with great expense, including among them many very learned men, yet not any of them have found anything: I answer, that this noble Art requires a sound man; all these have been sick; they have had the gold sickness, *which hath darkened their senses,* so that they could not understand the terms which the wise men use in the description of the Art; seeking only with hot desire that which they shall never find. But what is to be found, that they seek not; therefore they work in vain. Who is to be blamed, the Art or the Artist, that they understand nothing? Alchemy is a pure and uncorrupted virgin; she casts off the sensual man, and will have an intellectual one; of whom, at present, I see but few. Let no man's reason deceive him; we cannot be without errors, for very much of the idol hangeth on it. *In the Mind is the true Intellect,* which we must follow, not reason; so shall we enter, and thereby understand the wise men, who write rare things and easily know what it is...... The first operation of the Refiner [of man] is natural; the second, of the physician, is natural also; but the third is Divine; for God worketh here alone, and the physician standeth here in his stead."

Van Helmont also says, that Man is not well defined by *reason*, and insists that there is something in him above reason, which he calls religion. Van Suchten and Van Helmont probably both refer to that *something*, which the more modern phraseology places above the "understanding, judging according to sense"; a sort of intuition, which some have not hesitated to call an inspiration. This is what Van Suchten probably calls the *Mind*, and says it is not reason. Is it anything else than that *spiritual* sight which St. Paul says is necessary for discerning spiritual truths? The actual powers of man have always been the same, but as they are developed in individuals they take different names and give rise to controversies about mere words. That man has a power of *conceiving* truths which the senses cannot *perceive*, seems a mere matter of fact, about which there need be no difference of opinion. The real difficulty here is perhaps that of distinguishing *intuitions* from mere *imaginations*.

But I must return to Van Suchten, who says, after describing with extraordinary minuteness, though in figures, the new birth, that

"The physician [meaning Teacher] who hath not this knowledge, let him not meddle with *mercury* [for we have a warning of the consequences of the blind leading the blind], for it is not for him. But he who earnestly thirsteth after the knowledge of Nature, and is well experienced in chemistry [meaning the knowledge of man], may take mercury in hand. What I mention, seek therein; all is in it, [Know Thyself,] and if thou rightly goest about it, thou shalt experimentally find that which I have met with: then shalt thou see that I have written this Treatise, not out of hate or envy, but from a true heart, and for the lovers of truth; not according to my fancy and speculations, but from perfect experience, which time, according to God's will, hath manifested to me."

Who can imagine that this style of writing was used by a seeker after earthly riches? The author may be called a deluded fool, but no man in his senses can read this very grave little volume of Van Suchten's, and suppose that the writer was thinking of perishable treasures.

It is remarkable that all of the Alchemists denounce mere money-seekers. They promise the sons of Art riches indeed, but they are the "riches of the wisdom and knowledge of God." I admit, of course, that multitudes of the selfish and ignorant were led by their promises, literally understood, to seek among real metals for an agent for turning common metals into gold, and this class of men may unconsciously have prepared the way for modern chemistry; but it is not just to omit all notice of the genuine Alchemists, and affix to their Art the odium which only belongs to a class of people called "ignorant sots" by the Alchemists themselves. We have seen what Van Suchten says of those who were duped, or attempted to deceive others. Here is a passage from Eyrenæus:—

" Since, then, this knowledge is so wonderful, being *the very Looking-glass of Nature*, the antidote against poverty and sickness, and consequently the cut-throat of covetousness, pride, ambition, and such like sordid affections, who would not bestow a little time in the inquiry of it? In which, let me assure thee, in the very words of Trevisan, *the Art is so plain, that, if it were nakedly described, it would seem to be contemptible;* and yet in mechanical arts how frequent is it for men to serve seven, eight, yea, ten years' apprenticeship to attain them? And in some that are a little more ingenious, how frequently are considerable sums of money bestowed to boot; yet in this noble Art, excelling all human sciences, as the sun doth a candle, who will employ himself with diligence? unless it be some money-minded sots, who seek only for riches; and yet even they are soon weary. So that few or none persist in the inquiry, save a few roguish sophists who live by cozening; *by reason of whom the Art is scandalized*, and ill spoken of. Yet trust me, for I speak knowingly, the Art is both true and easy; yea, so easy, that, if you were to see the experiment, you would hardly believe it."

M. Figuier speaks of the causes of the overthrow of Alchemy, and, curiously enough, cites among others the labors of Otto Tachenius, giving him great credit therefor. The work of Tachenius is in two parts, the first, the *Hoppocrates chymicus*, was written against *false* Alchemists, and was intended to turn from the study all hasty and immature wits; but the *Clavis* annexed to it, as the second part, is a genuine alchemical work, and even the first part is strewed with Hermetic philosophy, purposely made impenetrable to dunces.

The celebrated Robert Boyle wrote a book ostensibly against certain supposed principles of the Alchemists; but he took care to approve and recommend, and even to explain and defend, mystically, — in their own jargon, — what he distinguished as their practical work. The truth is, that some, losing sight of the legitimate "Work," ambitiously sought to *explain* the Universe, and this, too, in a more or less mechanical sense. To this class of writers Mr. Boyle took just exception; but he stops far short of a condemnation of Alchemy.

A most remarkable Essay touching this subject may be seen in Bishop Berkeley's Iris, or Essay on *Tar Water*. Bishop Berkeley well knew the real object of the Alchemists, and had something more than sympathy for it, as any one may see who will understandingly read his Essay on Tar Water: Tar Water indeed!

Readers of metaphysical writings will recollect that Father Malebranche would have us "see all things in God," while Bishop Berkeley would have us recognize the Spirit of God in all things. Is the Spirit of God anything but God? What essential difference is there between these doctrines? To say that we see God in all things, or all things in God, is to say the same thing, provided these expressions have any meaning at all, and are not a mere form of words.

M. Figuier and the Reviewer make merry with the word *Alcahest*, or the *universal dissolvent*, "sought by all the experimentalists." "Of course," says the Reviewer, "many proclaimed that they had found it, until Kunkel scattered the whole fabric of pretension by a single phrase: 'What kind of vessel,' he asked, '*contains* this universal dissolvent?'" M. Figuier notices the derivation of the word in the German, *al-geist* (*all-Spirit*), but does not profit by it, and yet this amazingly obtuse-witted man has published what he calls an *historical and critical Essay* upon Hermetical Philosophy!

Bishop Berkeley knew very well what *Alcahest* meant in the writings of the Alchemists, and was far enough from denying the Spirit of God because no human vessel can be made to *contain* it, well seeing, nevertheless, that it is contained in all things. The Alchemists knew that it could not be contained, or rather confined, in a formula of words, and held up for the curiosity of the idle, much less for the profane; yet to the properly prepared and *purified* soul it is the most apparent thing in the universe.

Who shows the most reverence for God, — he who parades the name before his readers as he would that of a familiar acquaintance, or he who throws a veil over what he hopes he may not be mistaken in as a result of whole years of meditation upon his sacred name?

Let any one read the qualifications set out by Basil Valentine as necessary in him who would understand anything of *Antimony*, and consider to what they really point. There is something in the very title of his work, "The Triumphal Chariot of Antimony," which may remind us of the Chariot of Fire in the Book of Kings.

According to Basilius it is necessary, as a preparation for the study of *Antimony*, to make, —

"1st. Invocation to God, with a certain heavenly intention, drawn from the bottom of a pure and sincere heart and conscience, pure from all ambition, hypocrisy, and all other vices which have any affinity with these; as arrogance, boldness, pride, luxury, petulancy, oppression of the poor, and other similar evils, all of which are to be eradicated from the heart; that when a man desires to prostrate himself before the throne of grace, for obtaining health, he may do so with a conscience free from all unprofitable weeds, *that his body may be transmuted* into a holy temple of God, and be purged from all uncleanness. For God will not be mocked, (of which I would earnestly admonish all,) as worldly men, pleasing and flattering themselves with their own wisdom, think. God, I say, will not be mocked, but the Creator of all things will be invoked with reverential fear; and acknowledged with due obedience...... Which is so very true, that I am certainly assured no impious man shall ever be partaker of the true *medicine*, much less of the eternal heavenly bread. Therefore place your whole intention and trust in God; call upon him and pray that he may impart his blessing to you. Let this be the beginning of your work, that by the same you may obtain your desired end, and at length effect what you intended. For *the fear of the Lord is the beginning of wisdom.*"

After a whole page more to the same purpose, Basil comes to the *second* qualification, which he calls *Contemplation*, by which, says he, " I understand an accurate attention to the business itself, under which will fall these considerations, first to be noted. As, what are the circumstances of anything; what the matter; what the form; whence its operations proceed; whence it is infused and implanted; how generated"; etc., etc.; "also how the body of everything may be dissolved, that is, resolved into the *first matter*, or *first essence* (of which I have already made mention in other parts of my writings), *viz.* how the last matter may be changed into the first, and the first into the last. This contemplation," continues Basil, "is celestial, and to be understood with spiritual reason; for the circumstances and depth of things cannot be perceived in any other way than by the spiritual cogitation of man: and this contemplation is twofold. One is called possible, the other impossible. The latter consists in copious cogitations, which never proceed to effects, nor exhibit any form of matter that falls under the touch: as, if any one should endeavor to comprehend the Eternity of the Most High; which is vain and impossible; yea, it is a sin against the Holy Spirit, so arrogantly to pry into the Divinity itself, which is immense, infinite, and eternal; and to subject the incomprehensible counsel of the secrets of God to human inquisition. The other part of *Contemplation*, which is possible, is called *Theory*. This contemplates *that*, which is perceived by Touch and Sight, and hath a nature formed in Time: this considers, how that nature may be *helped and perfected* by resolution of itself; how *every body may give forth from itself the good or evil, venom or medicine, latent in it;* how destruction and confraction [to be cleft or opened] are to be handled, whereby under a right proceeding, without sophistical deceits, the pure may be severed and separated from the impure."

I must remind the reader to consider what Hollandus says of cleansing *Saturn*, and of what Van Suchten says of purifying Antimony; indeed, all of these writers hold but one language on this point, no matter what name they select for their *matter*, which everywhere, in all of the books, I say is *Man*, who is the subject of all this inquiry, all this labor, all this talk about the Philosopher's Stone. As a sample of what Basil says of the *qualifications* deemed important in a student of *Antimony*, I will cite the remainder of what he says under this head.

"This *Separation* is instituted and made by divers manual operations, and various ways; some of which are vulgarly known by experience, others remote from vulgar experience. These are calcination, sublimation, reverberation, circulation, putrefaction, digestion, distillation, cohobation, fixation, and the like of these; all the degrees of which are found in operating, learned, and perceived, and manifested by the same."

To caution the reader that some of these operations, though most real, are nevertheless invisible, and not the work of the hands, I would remind him to reflect upon what is said of a certain something which is sharper than any two-edged sword, piercing even to the dividing asunder of soul and spirit, and of the joints and marrow, and is a discerner of the thoughts and intent of the heart.

"Whence will clearly appear," continues Basil, "what is movable [transient], what is fixed [permanent], what is white, red, black, blue, or green, viz. when the operation is rightly instituted by the artificer; for possibly the operator may err, and turn aside from the right way; but *that Nature should err, when rightly handled, is not possible.*" I place this passage in italics, for I would have it noticed. "Therefore," says Basil, "if you shall err, so that nature cannot be altogether free, and released from the body, in which it is held captive, return again unto your way; learn the theory more perfectly, and inquire more accurately into the method of your operating, that you may discover the foundation and certainty in the separation of all things; which is a matter of great concern. And this is the second foundation of philosophy, which follows prayer; for in that the sum of the matter lies, and is contained in these words: Seek first the kingdom of God and his righteousness by prayer, and all other things shall be added unto you."

To show that Basil Valentine was not alone in thus denouncing the sort of preparation necessary for success in this study, I will recite a few of the *Canons* of Espagnet, viz.: —

"The light of this knowlege is the gift of God, which by his freeness he bestoweth upon whom he pleaseth. [The reader will remember the verse from John iii. 8.] Let none, therefore, set himself to the study hereof, until, having cleared and purified his heart, he devote himself wholly unto God, and be emptied of all affection to things impure."

"Those that are in public honors and offices, or be always busied with private and necessary occupations, let them not strive to attain to the top of this philosophy; for it requireth the whole man; and being found, possesseth him, and being possessed, challengeth him from all long and serious employments, esteeming all other things as strange unto him, and of no value." This language, it is true, is not quite so strong as that in Phil. iii. 8.

"Let him that is desirous of this knowledge clear his mind from all evil motions, especially pride, which is abomination to heaven, and the gate of hell. Let him be frequent at prayers, and charitable; have little to do with the world; abstain from too much company keeping, and enjoy constant tranquillity, that the mind may be able to reason more freely in, private, and be more highly lifted up; for unless it be kindled with a beam of divine light, it will hardly be able to penetrate the hidden mysteries of truth."

"A studious *Tyro* of a quick wit, constant mind, inflamed with the love of philosophy, very skilful in natural philosophy, of a pure heart, perfect in manners, mightily devoted to God, — even though ignorant of practical chemistry, — may with confidence enter the highway of Nature, and peruse the books of the best philosophers. Let him seek out an ingenious [and ingenuous] companion for himself, and not despair of accomplishing his desire."

It will be seen here, that for success in this study a knowledge of practical chemistry is not deemed indispensable. The reason is, that the subject is

Man, and a chief instrument in the work is *meditation*. It is not a work of the hands. Pontanus, a great name among the Alchemists, says he discovered the true Fire, after reading Artephius, by a "profound meditation," and affirms that it cannot be discovered in any other way.

"Let a Lover of Truth," continues Espagnet, "make use of but a few authors, but of best note and experienced truth; let him suspect things that are quickly understood, especially in *mystical names and secret operations;* for truth lies hid in obscurity; nor do philosophers ever write more deceitfully than when plainly, nor ever more truly than when obscurely."

Espagnet then recommends the works of Hermes, Morienus Romanus, Count Trevisan, and Raymond Lully; to which I would by all means add his own little book entitled *Arcanum, or the Grand Secret of Hermetical Philosophy*. He adds, in recommendation of Sandivogius: "As for that clear water sought for by many, found out by few, yet obvious and profitable unto all, which is the *base* of the philosopher's work, a noble *Polonian*, not more famous for his learning than subtlety of wit, (anonymous, whose name, nevertheless, a double anagram hath betrayed,) in his *Novum Lumen*

Chemicum, Parabola, and *Enigma,* as also in his Tract of *Sulphur,* hath spoken largely and freely enough; yea, he hath expressed all things concerning it so plainly, that nothing can be satisfactory to him that desireth more."

The reader has now before him, at what I fear he may consider a tedious length, extracts from Isaac Hollandus, Artephius, Van Suchten, Basil Valentine, and Espagnet, all well-known names of Alchemists, three of them especially referred to by the Reviewer as in pursuit of an agent for transmuting common metals into gold, and can hardly fail to see one pervading doctrine, explicable only by a due knowledge of the nature of man. I might easily add extracts from the works of more than a hundred other writers if it were necessary, and show, by slight explanatory notes, that every genuine Alchemist wrote only of Man. This is the class of men overlooked by the historian, who has fastened upon the weak and ignorant, or upon "impostors and mountebanks," as if these were the originators of Alchemy, when, so far from belonging to the class of those who entered into or sought to enter into the new birth, they properly belong to that production known among midwives as the *placenta.*

That chemistry is indirectly indebted to the Alchemists for its introduction among the sciences, is certainly true; at least, I have no disposition to question it; but not to the immediate labors of the Alchemists themselves, whose peculiar work was one of contemplation, and not a work of the hands. Their alembic, furnace, cucurbit, retort, philosophical egg, etc., etc., in which the work of fermentation, distillation, extraction of essences and spirits, and the preparation of salts is said to have taken place, was *Man*, — yourself, friendly reader, and if you will take yourself into your own study, and be candid and honest, acknowledging no other guide or authority but Truth, you may easily discover something of Hermetic Philosophy; and if at the beginning there should be " fear and trembling," the end may be a more than compensating peace.

It is a plain case, that, for the most part, the experiments which led the way to chemistry were made by men who were misled by the language of the Alchemists, and sought gold instead of truth; but this class of men wrote no books upon Alchemy. Many of them no doubt died over their furnaces, "*uttering no voice*," and none of them wrote books upon the Philosopher's Stone, for the simple reason that they never discovered anything to write about, and were incapable of indicating in the remotest manner any method for its discovery. I know that some impostors purposely wrote of mysteries to play upon the credulity of the ignorant; but their works have nothing alchemical about them. It is true, also, that many books were written by men who really imagined they had discovered the secret, and were nevertheless mistaken. But this imaginary success could never have had place where *gold* was the object; because in the *bald fact* no man was ever deceived: no man ever believed that he had discovered a method of making gold out of inferior metals. The thing speaks for itself. It is impossible that any man can ever be deluded upon this bare fact; but it is quite otherwise with respect to the real object of Alchemy, in which men have been deceived in all ages, either under the name of Alchemy, or under some other name;— for the *subject* is always in the world, and hence the antiquity claimed for the art by the Alchemists. Upon this subject, and I admit, under the name of Alchemy, many mistaken men have written large volumes, for I have some of them; and to a novice these works are among the obstacles in the study, for until some skill is obtained, the student has no rule for separating the chaff from the wheat.

To a man who cannot read at all, all books are alike; and to one who reads in but one language, by much the greater part of the books in the world are incomprehensible; while of the books in the language one reads, those only come within his comprehension up to near the level of which he has risen by cultivation, study, and research. D'Alembert congratulated himself that his works on *Mathematics* could not be criticised by fools.

The Reviewer gives the opinion, that the religious language found in books of Alchemy was not in use among the Arabs who sought the Philosopher's Stone, but was introduced by Christians after the subject was transferred to Christendom; when, he says, religious *inspiration* was believed to be necessary for the discovery of the agent for transmuting metals; the Reviewer still being under the impression that gold was the object. He says that this *religious language* is all that gives "a sort of pretext" to the views in my pamphlet.

If the writer of the article in the Westminster Review should by any chance ever fall in with this defence of the Alchemists, not of myself, I beg him to believe that I do not tax him with an inability to perceive his error, if he would consult the works of the Alchemists. My only surprise is that he should have ventured upon the subject so illy prepared for it. If he will look into the writings of Geber the Arabian, his eye may chance to fall upon such passages as the following: —

"We have described it [the Stone] in such a way of speaking, as is agreeable to the will of the Most High, Blessed, Sublime, and Glorious God, and our own mind. We have written the same, as it happened to be recollected, or as it was infused by *the grace of his Divine goodness, who gives it to, and withholds it from, whom he will.*"

And again: "The Artist should be intent on the true *End* only, because our Art is reserved in the *Divine Will of God*, and is given to, or withheld from, whom he will; who is glorious, sublime, and full of justice and goodness."

It will be difficult to discover in this language any other than the religious spirit which the Reviewer thinks was introduced after the subject had been transferred into Christendom.

The Reviewer also says that the Arabians never thought of the Philosopher's Stone as a cure for diseases; and yet the same Geber speaks of it as a "medicine, rejoicing and preserving the Body in youth."

This is alchemical language for expressing immortality, and if any one wishes to speak of this under the rose, how can it be better represented than as perpetual youth?

Geber further gives the student this instruction: "Dispose yourself by exercise to the study with great industry and labor, and a *continued deep meditation;* for *by these you may find it, and not otherwise.*"

What can meditation do with actual metals? It cannot blow the coals under an alembic; but it may bring a man into a right state for hearing the still, small voice, whose potency, like that of the *Alcahest*, — for it is the Alcahest, — is able to dissolve the stoniest hearts.

Again, Geber says: — "If we have concealed anything, [meaning by enigmatical writing,] ye sons of learning, wonder not, for we have not concealed it from you, but have delivered it in such language as that it may be hid from evil men, and that the unjust and vile might not know it. But, ye sons of Truth, search, and you shall find this most excellent gift of God, which he has reserved for you"; — as if he had expressly the language of Scripture in view, — " Seek, and ye shall find; knock, and it shall be opened unto you." But he adds: —

" Ye sons of folly, impiety, and profanity, avoid you the seeking after this knowledge; it will be destructive to you, and precipitate you into contempt and misery. This gift of God is absolutely, by the judgment of the Divine Providence, hid from you, and denied you for ever.

" Perhaps for the punishment of your sophistical work, God denies you the Art, and lamentably thrusts you into the by-path of error, and from your error into perpetual infelicity and wretchedness; for he is most miserable and unhappy, to whom, after the end of his work and labor, God denies the sight of Truth. For such a man is doomed to perpetual labor, beset with misfortune and infelicity, loseth the consolation, joy, and delight of his life, and consumes his whole time in grief without profit."

Who can read such language, and suppose that the author was thinking of gold? He was not! He was writing of the Truth: and this is *Geber* the *Arabian*.

The Reviewer is not less unfortunate in his reference to George Ripley, a monk of the fifteenth century. Ripley's *Compound of Alchemy*, only one of many works by him on the same subject, became a text-book for the Alchemists, who continually refer to it with eulogy. It would be tedious, or, by a few extracts, it might be easily shown that Ripley wrote only of man, and never dreamed of making gold in any other sense than that of making goodness.

The Reviewer thinks that Ripley publicly recanted his errors in Alchemy, and endeavored to dissuade others from falling into similar errors. This story evidently arose from the urgent dissuasives against *false* Alchemy, contained in some of his works, where he warns every one against endeavors to discover the secret by working in common metals and minerals, enumerating in his compound of Alchemy a whole page full of *things* in which the secret cannot be found;—because, in short, it is not a work of the hands at all, but the product of a certain divine contemplation, productive rather of a state of *being* than one of mere *knowing*, or of knowing as a consequence of being in a particular state.

Many of the writers, especially Pontanus, Eyrenæus, and Espagnet, as also Ripley, just named, warn their readers not to lose their time, money, and labor in working with common metals;—which may be taken very literally, or it may be construed as applying to a certain class of common men who either cannot or will not receive instruction. But these warnings were thrown away upon a multitude of self-seekers, who desired not the kingdom of God, but were intent upon earthly riches.

Since my curiosity was awakened on this subject, I have gathered over two hundred works on Alchemy and Hermetic Philosophy, judging by a glance at my book-shelves, and I confess that I have read them with the best attention in my power, and with a continually increasing interest. If I felt called upon to justify this sort of reading, I might refer to the declarations of Schelling. After this great German philosopher had exhausted all sorts of recognized treatises upon philosophy, he confessed that he found more "fulness and great heart-language" in Jacob Behmen, than in all of them put together; and Jacob Behmen was an Alchemist, though very far from among the best of them.

But no Alchemist supports his views by appeals to authority. He would have every doctrine tested by "the possibility of nature," and repudiates the practice of testing nature by authority. The Alchemist settles no question by an *ipse dixit*, or "the master has said it." He acknowledges "no master but one," unless, in the spirit of 1 Cor. xv. 27, 28, he would have all things brought to the standard of truth, but truth must be submitted to God, who is All in All.

I have endeavored, as the reader will please notice, to point out chiefly *the base*, or introduction to Alchemy; and have not been disposed to say much of *the end*, which, it is easy to see, must be developed in the experience of those who put themselves in a condition for it. If any man would realize the blessings of goodness, he must become good; or if he would enjoy the advantages of truth, he must be true. There is no mystery in this, and yet this is good Alchemy, so far as it goes.

It is contended that the real doctrine of the Alchemists lies within the field of human nature. They find their principles in the common life of man, and acknowledge that "many honest men of good consciences and affections do secretly enjoy this gift of God." The chief peculiarity about it is, that it takes up some of the most universally experienced instincts of man, relating to every-day duties, such as many honest men practise unconsciously, and erects them into a doctrine of life, and finds *Sanctions* in the reality of the instincts and experiences, without building upon any mere passion whatever.

I admit, however, that there are references to mysteries in the writings of the Alchemists, about which I have no wish to speak at length. Some of the writers, for example, say that no true philosopher, *who knew it*, has ever named, or will ever name, what they call the *First Matter*, — as if this was not a name!

When I say that *Man* is the *subject* upon which the Alchemists employ themselves, I do not mean to say that the phenomenal Man is what they call the *First Matter*. This word, I presume, expresses a conception which cannot be put into descriptive language without compromising to some extent the feelings of awe with which the Supreme Being should ever be contemplated, and I am therefore disposed to think, on this account as well as for some other reasons, that, whether there is or is not a Hermetic Philosophy *by name* still in the world, the Art, or whatever it may be called, will always remain among men. Perhaps the answer to the question, " Tell me thy Name ? " will always reduce to silence him who receives it, though this may remain for ever the one question which "lies at the bottom of every human heart."

Although it is said that the pure in heart shall see God, there is a sense, no doubt, in which it is true that no man can see God and live. There is no one of our senses more adapted to metaphorical use than that of sight; and, assuredly, when men "see into the life of things," they do not use the outward sense. Two of the greatest poets the world has seen, who *saw* most clearly into the nature of things, were blind.

There may be very good reasons to justify the Hindoos in never pronouncing audibly their mystic word *AUM*, and the same reasons explain why they have no image and pay no worship directly to *Brahm*, though they have altars to Brahma, Siva, and Vishnu, and a multitude of other divinities. We do ourselves wrong, not them, when we fail to recognize the reverence implied in this.

The Hermetic Philosophers claim a perfect harmony with each other, but this harmony is confined to a few principles of vital importance in their doctrine, which relate almost wholly to a certain *practice;* — possibly a complete application of the notion of duty, as explained by Kant, writing of his celebrated "categorical imperative," or "apodictic command"; — an unreasoning, though not unreasonable, obedience to an experienced imperious sense of duty, leaving the result to God; and this I am disposed to call *the Way.*

Now *the End* is, perhaps, the fruit of this obedience. The man, by a steady preservation of the inward unity, being prepared alike for all outward events, may finally be the subject of some special experience by which a seal of confirmation is set upon what at first was a certain divine trust in the ultimate blessing of rectitude. I suppose it to involve a peculiar knowledge of the unity of God, with a sense of participation in it; for, God being "perfect truth and perfect love," it follows, with some appearance of mathematical certainty, that if a man can enter into a life of truth and love, he really enters into the life of God, and must feel, conversely, that the life of God has entered into him. The lesser magnet becomes perfectly adjusted, and rests in the greater magnet.

In this state men who may never have heard of Alchemy, for a life of truth and goodness depends upon God and not upon books, have written volumes with the title, *The Life of God in the Soul of Man.*

This may be the union of the human and divine so much insisted upon by both philosophers and divines, and be itself the seal of salvation. Allusions to this state are everywhere met with in sacred literature, as an example of which I take the following from the Rev. John Norris, — writing about 1690.

"These supposals," says he, "being premised, — first, that that Truth which is perfective is necessary Truth; then, secondly, that this necessary Truth is the same with the Divine Ideas; then, thirdly, that the Divine *Nous*, or Eternal Wisdom, is intrinsically with or præsential to the Mind; then, fourthly, that we see and understand all things [that we properly understand] in him, and that 't is He that enlightens us; and that lastly, though he enlightens all *Fundamentally and Potentially*, yet this illumination is not reduced into *act*, and made *effectual*, but by the intervention of some condition on our parts, which is duly to consult and apply ourselves to Him: — from these premises, I say, it necessarily and evidently follows, that the right and only method of inquiry after that Truth which is perfective, is to consult the Divine *Nous*, or Eternal Wisdom. For this is the region of Truth, and here are hid all the Treasures of Wisdom and Knowledge.

"This is that great and universal *Oracle* lodged in every man's breast, whereof the ancient Urim and Thummim was an expressive Type and Symbol. This is *Reason;* this is *Conscience;* this is *Truth;* this is that Light within, so darkly talked of by some who have, by their awkward, untoward, and unskilful way of representing it, discredited one of the noblest theories in the world. But the thing in itself, rightly understood, is true; and if any man shall yet call it Quakerism or Enthusiasm, I shall only make this reply at present, that it is such Quakerism as makes a good part of St. John's Gospel and of St. Augustine's works. But to return; this, I say, is the *Divine Oracle* which we all may and must consult, if we would enrich our minds with Truth, — that Truth which is perfective of the understanding. And this is the method of being truly wise. And this method is no other than what is advised us by the Divine *Nous*, the substantial wisdom of God (Prov. viii. 34): 'Blessed is the man that heareth me, watching daily at my gates, waiting at the posts of my doors'; and again, says the same substantial wisdom (ch. ix. 4) : 'Whoso is simple [honest], let him turn in hither'; and again (John viii. 12) : 'I am the light of the world; he that follows me' (or, as the word moré properly signifies, he that consorts or keeps company with me) 'walketh not in darkness.'

"This, therefore, is the *via intelligentiæ, the way and method of true knowledge,*—to apply ourselves to the Divine *Nous,* the eternal wisdom of God,"— which Dr. Norris had just expressed by the word *conscience.*

This I regard as good Alchemy, without the name. The application only requires that it shall be complete, thorough, and entire, for its practice requires "the whole man."

When I turned to this passage, I did not perceive at first that Dr. Norris had spoken of the conscience as *the Way*,—answering precisely to the view I have been endeavoring to present.

The Rev. Mr. Norris, it is true, raised a storm around his ears by his tendency to Platonism and Quakerism, though he thought it good St. Johnism. Some one took the pains to write a book to ridicule his views of the "ideal and intelligible world," and he was called, as usual in such cases, a *Mystic*. Men who live principally in the sensuous world can never forgive those who take the hint from the melting of a piece of ice, and think it possible that

> " The cloud-capped towers, the gorgeous palaces,
> The solemn temples, the great globe itself,
> Yea, all which it inherit, shall dissolve " ; —

and then, by devout contemplation, reach a conviction that, notwithstanding the perishable nature of all outward existences, there is an invisible, imperishable reality "prepared from the foundation of the world" for those who properly prepare themselves for it, and that this is the only *real* reality in existence.

But to return to the Philosophers: — although they lean upon the conscience as *the Way*, or as the "base" of the work, they rely chiefly upon *Love* as working the greatest of wonders, that of a transformation of the *subject* of it into the *object loved*. We may occasionally meet with detached passages where special opinions are expressed without a systematic purpose, which, nevertheless, may easily be adjusted to the more elaborately stated doctrine under figures and allegories. One of these I find in these words: —

"I find the nature of Divine Love to be a perfect unity and simplicity. There is nothing more one, undivided, simple, pure, unmixed, and uncompounded than Love. *You will ask, how this can be proved? Very well:* for this Love is God himself [1 John iv. 8]: now there is nothing more essential to God than Unity and Simplicity; nothing more contrary to the Divine Nature than duality, division, or composition. Besides, it is this Love which gives unity and harmony to all things. There is no unity in Heaven nor on Earth, but what is derived from Love, and must acknowledge Him for its author; and do you think that Love can want that unity which it gives to all others? No, certainly; rather conclude, that that which makes all things one, which harmonizeth and agrees the most different and discordant natures, must needs be unity itself.

"In the second place I find Love to be the most perfect and absolute liberty. Nothing can move Love, but Love; nothing touch Love, but Love; nor nothing constrain Love, but Love. It is free from all things; itself only gives laws to itself, and those laws are the laws of Liberty; for nothing acts more freely than Love, because it always acts from itself, and is moved by itself; by which prerogatives Love shows himself allied to the Divine Nature, yea, to be God himself.

"Thirdly, Love is all strength and power. Make a diligent search through Heaven and Earth, and you will find nothing so powerful as Love. What is stronger than Hell and Death? Yet Love is the triumphant conqueror of both. What more formidable than the wrath of God? Yet Love overcomes it, and dissolves and changes it into itself. In a word, nothing can withstand the prevailing strength of Love: it is the strength of Mount Zion, which can never be moved.

"In the fourth place: Love is of a transmuting and transforming nature. The great effect of Love is to turn all things into its own nature, which is all goodness, sweetness, and perfection. This is that Divine power which turns water into wine; sorrow and anguish into exulting and triumphant joy; and curses into blessings. Where it meets with a barren and heathy desert, it *transmutes* it into a paradise of delights; yea, it changeth evil into good, and all imperfection into perfection. It restores that which is fallen and degenerated to its primary beauty, excellence, and perfection. It is the *Divine Stone, the White Stone with the name written upon it, which no one knows but he that hath it.* In a word, it is the Divine Nature, it is God himself, whose essential property it is to assimilate all things with himself; or (if you will have it in the Scripture phrase) to *reconcile all things to himself, whether they be in Heaven or in Earth;* and all by means of this Divine Elixir, whose transforming power and efficacy nothing can withstand."

In reading such passages, written by an Alchemist, a reader of alchemical books readily thinks of the language employed upon a certain *Mercury* extracted from *Saturn* (or Antimony, &c., &c.), in which is sown a certain *philosophical gold*, and readily concludes, that, while the first refers to an awakening of the conscience which withdraws the subject of it from the entanglements of a merely worldly life, the second is the Divine Love engrafted upon it which binds the soul eternally to God.

While it exists as an *affection* it may be what is called "our" *Luna*, and the "White" state of the Stone, for the Stone is Man. The course of nature seems to be relied upon as sufficient to carry the subject of this affection to a more or less distinct consciousness of the Unity of all things, which, becoming an intellectual conviction, may be called *Sol*, or the *Red* State of the Stone.

All of the writers speak of three principal *colors* in the Stone, Black, White, and Red. If the white and red states be supposed hinted at above, the Black, I take it, is what I have suggested in my pamphlet, — a certain *humility*, which Pontanus calls *a philosophical contrition*, which does not necessarily suppose actual guilt, but only a sense of that purity, in the presence of which the angels veil their faces as unworthy to look upon it. It may be found very accurately described in Goethe's *Confessions of a Fair Saint*.

As an intellectual result, there seems nothing more insisted upon in alchemical books than the Unity; yet all Alchemists insist also upon a Trinity. In the Microcosm it may be considered as imaged by the Body, Soul, and Spirit. It may somewhat illustrate the subject, so far as man represents it, to refer to the common language by which man says, *I have a Soul;* and again, *I have a Body;* in which double expressions the *I* may stand for the Unity of the other two, but the expressions ought to be I *am* a Soul, and I *am* a Body.

Some of the writers might possibly lead their

readers to such notions as may be expressed by speaking first of God as Self-existence; then of God regarded as *Active* (cause), and then of God as Passive (effect); and finally to conceive these three as One; for while a cause implies necessarily an effect, an effect no less implies a cause; while both cause and effect imply necessary existence.

A good deal is said of a certain (which many may think always means a very uncertain) *middle* substance, — "which is to be taken," say some of the writers. This expression implies a Trinity, for there can be no middle without extremes; and so, again, there can be no extremes without a middle, and no one extreme without another. This is illustrated in Plato's *Statesman*, under the words moderation, excess, and deficiency, where *Moderation* is treated as the regulating, self-balancing *permanent* in the ever-variable extremes. It may be regarded as the scientific view of the celebrated poetic *in media*, &c., where alone is found what a modern writer has very happily called the *animated repose* of nature.

Whatever be the mode of it, the Hermetic writers all indicate some doctrine of the Trinity, yet on no account is this suffered to veil the Unity. They sometimes speak of three inseparable or co-existing *principles*, and say that either one of the three may be conceived as *the base* of the other two, which then, relatively only, are regarded as "Superficial"; as, the notion of Father implies that of Son; but the idea of the Son no less posits that of the Father; while the two presuppose a nature common to both.

In a somewhat similar manner, an essence supposes existence, while existence supposes essence. "One is not without the other," says Swedenborg; whence, though the language may seem unusual at first, it might be said that God is the essence of Nature, while Nature is the existence of God, and yet inseparable in unity. And here, if it should be asked what is the *nature* of God, the answer might be, it is nature itself; for nature is not the nature of anything but of God, whose essence is nevertheless invisible, while his existence is altogether and absolutely undeniable.

In a somewhat similar manner, every *subject* in nature may be regarded in a twofold point of view; as it is in its principles (substantially) and as it is in manifestation (phenomenally). Thus Water, Air, Light, &c. are variable, fluctuating things, phenomenally considered; but the sciences of hydrostatics, pneumatics, and optics, drawn from these *subjects*, express the unchangeable laws according to which the phenomena take place; yet the permanent and the transient are inseparable in all of them; and if the whole of nature be considered as one *subject*, it may be conceived, from this view, as permanent in its laws, that is, in its science; but variable, phenomenally, to the senses: but the two are inseparable, and in the expressions, one nature, one science, and one manifestation, we find a Trinity.

In the view expressed by Swedenborg I find something similar, for he says that there is a Trinity in all things, which he calls *end*, *cause*, and *effect*; saying that the effect is a manifestation (what Van Helmont calls an out-birth) of the *End*, as existing in the Idea of God, the Unity and *Cause* of all. Each of these ideas is correlative, and supposes the other two; and hence it would seem to be impossible for man to deny either the Unity or Trinity, a right conception of which may be the most important idea a philosopher can reach, though in its attainment he may be compelled to undergo a complete revolution of ordinarily received educational notions usually laid upon the sensuous organism, without penetrating, indeed, to any great depth. In this view, every discovery in science — for science is a discovery, and not an invention — is an entrance into a knowledge of God's essence by means of which man enters upon the control of nature; for nature is subjected to man's control only by a knowledge of its unchangeable principles or laws, by means of which it becomes obedient of the art of man, which nevertheless is subordinate to nature, contrary to which art can accomplish nothing.

This I take to be the sense of Lord Bacon, — Sir Francis and not the Friar, — where he says: "Man, as a minister and interpreter of Nature, does and understands as much as his observations on the *order* of Nature, either with regard to things *or the mind,* permit him; and neither knows nor is capable of more."

In one of my Alchemical volumes, I find *Art* is defined as *nature working through man;* and we read in Shakespeare: —

>"*Perdita.* I have heard it said,
>There is an art, which, in their piedness, shares
>With great creating Nature.
>   "*Polixenes.* Say, there be;
>Yet nature is made better by no *mean,*
>But nature makes that *mean:* so, o'er that art,

Which, you say, adds to nature, is an art
That nature makes. You see, sweet maid, we marry
A gentler scion to the wildest stock;
And make conceive a bark of baser kind
By bud of nobler race. This is an art
Which does mend nature, — change it rather; but
The art itself is nature."

But I insist upon nothing upon this subject, and will in patience bide my time; meanwhile adopting the doctrine of Socrates, not to think I know what I do not know. Still I will repeat that a notion of the Unity, in some sense, seems important with the Alchemists, a number of whom endeavor to indicate a method of arriving at a knowledge of it, which seems, with them, the principle of what they call the "fixation" of the matter of the Stone, for no man can attain to a unity in himself while drawn in opposite directions by principles out of harmony with each other. "No man can serve two masters."

If, now, *Love* be a prevailing cause in bringing about this unity in man both with himself and with God, — and one cannot be without the other; and if this be the "philosophic gold" we read of in books of Hermetic Philosophy; and if this Love cannot take root except in a conscience purged of all "superfluities," and yet is something common to all men; and if this *purgation* is not genuine except it arises in the subject, as proper to it, in order to a preservation and not a destruction of the specific nature of the subject, — then, I think, I have a glimpse of what may be called a theory for the explanation of alchemic books, and may form some remote opinion of the so earnestly sought Philosopher's Stone, before which all contradictions in life disappear. Here are the waters of Zemzem, this is the great elixir, and this the universal medicine; yet the students of this divine science, as the writers call it, are now universally regarded as having devoted their lives to the perishable treasures of the world. That they have brought this reputation upon themselves, by their mystical and symbolic language, is very certain; yet, however much they might have been mistaken, there seems no reason now, in this "enlightened age," why some attempt should not be made to show them as they were, in pursuit of the one thing needful, be it what it may.

I would be thought strenuous in setting forth what I call *the way* to the Philosopher's Stone, and yet there is not wanting a variety in the modes adopted for carrying the student to a comprehension of the mysteries about which the writers employ themselves.

Eyræneus Philalethes, sometimes called Cosmopolita, for he wrote under both names, in one place, I think, points very plainly to the two processes, *analysis* and *synthesis*, both of which have one end. To seek the Unity through Sol, I take it, is to employ the intellect upon the *Idea* of the Unity, by analysis to terminate in the parts; whereas to study upon Mercury, here used for nature at large, is to work synthetically, and, by combining the parts, reach an idea of the Unity. The two lead to the same thing, beginning as it were from opposite extremes; for the analysis of any one thing, completely made, must terminate in the parts, while the parts, upon a synthetical reconstruction, must reproduce the Unity. One of the two ways indicated by Eyræneus is spoken of as a Herculean labor, which I suppose to be the second, the reconstruction of a unity by a recombination of the parts, which, in respect to nature, is undoubtedly a Herculean undertaking. The more hopeful method is by meditation under the preparation pointed out so clearly by Basil Valentine.

Some of the writers tell us to put " one of the Bodies into the Alembic," that is, — for this is what is meant, — take the Soul into the thought or study, and apply the *fire* (of intellect) to it until it "comes over" into spirit. Then, "putting this by for use," put in "the other Body," which is to be subjected to a similar trial until it "comes over" also; after which the two may be united, being found essentially or substantially the same. Such experiments are not intended for novices.

Others point out some sort of affinity between the Spirit and the Soul, and then undertake to show a similar affinity between the Soul and the Body, and thus carry the mind (?) to a recognition, in some way, of a mutual and inseparable interdependence of all upon all. But this is all done in figures and symbols.

This is a very strange mode of dealing with metaphysical questions, but no one will ever know anything of the import of the books of Hermetic Philosophy who shuts his mind to it, and persists in the vulgar opinion that the Alchemists were in pursuit of gold.

Whoever examines the "Six Keys," published at the end of the Hermetic Triumph (an excellent work, by the way), may discover that the *Third Key* is the explanation of the Unity, but, of course, in the usual veiled language. An every-day reader, or one who reads for amusement, would not gather a single idea from the perusal of those "Six Keyes," but a student, "germane to the matter," after repeated perusals, in connection with other books treating of the same subject, may at least discover enough to perceive the general object of the author, and cannot fail to conclude that, whatever he was writing about, it was not gold.

The passage cited by the Reviewer, in which some writer instructs a pupil, — "Je vous commande, fils de doctrine, congelez l'argent vif. De plusieurs choses faites, 2, 3, et 3, 1, 1 avec 3 c'est 4, 3, 2, et 1. De 4 à 3 il 7 a 1; de 3 à 4 il 7 a 1, donc 1 et 1, 3 et 4; de 3 à 1 il 7 a 2; de 2 à 3 il 7 a 1. Je vous ai tout dit," — is an attempt, very blind I confess, to lead the student to some notion of the universal unity; — how, from a beginning, which nevertheless has no commencement, all things were separated into "2," which the serious student may, if he chooses, consider the heavens and the earth, when yet "the earth was without form and void, and darkness was upon the face of the deep." Out of this chaos, by the word of God, was brought, order, system, and harmony. So is it, say these writers, in the "great work." Men are not born into a sense of the Unity, intellectually or otherwise, but of the "Many," which, as the crowning end of discipline, is to be conceived in Unity.

"The knowledge of the first member, of the Unity," says Socrates in the Seventh Book of the Republic, "is one of the things that exalt the mind, and, by separating it from sensuous things, leads it to the contemplation of that which *is*."

The Alchemists were of the opinion, that the knowledge of the One cannot be directly taught, and this was the opinion of Plato, as it is of many modern divines of the highest learning and genius, and those who hold this opinion lose sight of their own principles when they attempt directly to teach it. They resort therefore to numbers, figures, and allegories. The particular passage above cited from the Review, especially signalized by M. Figuier, had no other design than to indicate the progress of things to Unity, most likely by a student of the Pythagorean system, where much is made of 1, 2, 3, 4, and 7. I have noticed it, not to recommend it, but in order, by pointing at the intent of it, to show that it was not invented by a seeker after gold, but by some one who probably held the Unity to be ineffable, and that it can only be indicated by shadows and similitudes, while yet a true knowledge of it is "all" one needs, because, in short, it is the knowledge of God, who is All in All. Such passages, held up to ridicule by the Reviewer, ought not to be considered alone, but should be read in connection with entire works on the subject, in which one part may throw light upon every other. The books are everywhere filled with enigmas "hard to be understood," but with patience and application a student will meet with a great deal, if not entire satisfaction. Every position or opinion found in these works is expressed enigmatically, as witness what Basil says of the Unicorn's-horn, where the Unity is indicated, and with it, the doctrine of its freedom from evil, it being in its nature incapable of it.

Van Helmont, to teach that more can be accomplished by following nature than by attempting to force nature to follow us, gravely tells a story of two ships being built, upon one of which the plank was laid with the top ends, as they grew in the tree, towards the bow, while upon the other they were nailed without regard to this principle; and he tells us that the first was by far the best sailer. Van Helmont's readers may remember a remarkable story of a man who had a *nose* supplied from the arm of another man, who submitted to an operation for a consideration. The nose answered very well for a time, and appeared quite natural; but one day, suddenly, in Strasburg I believe it was, the *nose fell off;* it was soon after ascertained that the original owner of the nose had died coincident with the loss of it. Van Helmont meant to teach that doctrines of time perish with their sources. This was all he intended by that strange story.

This mode of teaching may be stigmatized as trivial and ridiculous; but whoever denounces it ought at least to understand the object of it. Hermetic Philosophy, so far as it is philosophy at all, is nothing but the truth of nature clothed or set out under a veil; that is, hid in figures, symbols, and enigmas. It obliges the student to appeal to the source of it, and what cannot be found there may and should be neglected, or at least held in reserve.

Norton, in the fifth chapter of his *Ordinall*, refers to the *Seven* virtues for amending the "faults" of man as follows: — the virtues being the four cardinal virtues, — prudence, temperance, fortitude, and justice; and the three theological virtues, — faith, hope, and charity.

"Moreover it helpeth in Alchemy,
To know Seven waters effectually;

Which be copied with many a man;
While they be common, seek them as ye can;
Desire not this Book to show things all,
For this book is but an *Ordinall.*
By those *Waters* men weene in mind
All *faults* to amend of *metaline kind.*

. . . . .

For they suppose with confidence unfeigned,
That all virtues requisite in them be contained;
Some to mollify Metals hard wrought,
And some to harden Metals that be soft," &c., &c.

I suppose it must be admitted that books of Alchemy had no charms for the so-called general reader, who required pictorial scenes for the fancy, or occasions for sentiment; but as for thinking, that was too much of a task, and must be had at second hand. This sort of writing was never intended for ordinary readers; but now, as the age is gone by when such books were written, it is surely interesting to learn how men of thought communicated with each other all over Europe, by means of a conventional language, forced into existence and use, in part, no doubt, by the persecution to which all free thought was exposed. The language was called by those who used it *Lingua magica, Lingua Angelorum,* and sometimes *Lingua ipsius Ternarii Sancti,*— in the use of which the writers admit that all who attempted it were not equally successful. One small work has this significant title: *Zoroaster's Cave; or, The Philosophers' Intellectual Echo to one another from their Cells.*

This Compendium of the "Work" opens abruptly thus:—

"Dry water from the Philosopher's clouds! Look for it, and be sure to have it, for it is the key to inaccessibles and to those *Locks* that would otherwise keep thee out.

"It is a middle nature between Fixed and Not Fixed, and partakes of a Sulphur *Azurine.*

"It is a raw, cooling, feminine Fire, and expects its impregnation from a Masculine, Solar Sulphur."

The interpretation of this, according to the view I take of Alchemy, is simply this:— A pure conscience (or a pure heart),— look for it, and be sure to have it, for it is the key, &c. It is of a middle nature between Soul and Body, and partakes of a heavenly spirit. It expects (or will receive) life from God (and the birth is Love and Unity).

This little work says: "Our water (the Antimonial Vinegar of Artephius) is a lustral, or expiating essence, and the cause efficient of the charity of the whole Body, and medicine. Two things it works in the Earth [i. e. in man]: it washes it; it tinges it: as it washes, it is Water; as it tinges, it is Air."

The reader may easily see how these writers enjoin upon all who seek the Truth a pure heart, as a preparation for an entrance into high experiences. They tell us the latter is not possible without the former; — as if acting upon the principle that everything in the universe has its proper "cause efficient," without which the effect cannot follow. The simplicity of the doctrine ought not to be an objection to it. There are mysteries enough independently of it.

There are many signs in alchemical volumes of a Secret Society, in which possibly the language used was conventionally determined. I have at times thought that some members of the Masonic fraternity might have found the secret language of the Alchemists a convenient mode of publishing, or rather of circulating among the initiated, doctrines of which they had taken "an oath" not to speak directly, or to make known except to a brother.

It is quite certain that books in a mysterious language were written by members of the Rosicrucian Society, who, I think it would be easy to show, had agreed to speak and write of each other before the uninitiated as sylphs, fairies, elfs, gnomes, and salamanders. The small volume under the title of the *Comte de Gabalis*, I am persuaded, was written by a Rosicrucian, and exhibits something of the manner by which the members of that fraternity approached strangers, and sounded them upon the subject of becoming members. The work was well known in its day, and has made some talk recently, but it is not the work of an Alchemist.

Whatever may be the fact with regard to some of the books, as *excrescences*, having some appearance of belonging to the class of Hermetic works, but without value, there can be no doubt of the antiquity of the subject, or of the enigmatical mode of treating it. This would still be true, even admitting that the works under the name of Hermes are all supposititious. It can never be ascertained who wrote the *Smaragdine Table*, or when it was written; but, for all practical purposes, such questions are of no importance; because the point always is, not as to the authorship, but as to the truth of the doctrines published.

Questions of science cannot be determined upon testimony except for the unscientific, who must receive upon trust what they are incapable of verifying by an appeal to what are called first principles.

In matters of history, where testimony to *facts* is important, it is otherwise. In this case, the veracity and competency in judgment of the historian must be established, or the facts recorded may be looked upon as comparatively unimportant.

But no question dependent upon outward testimony for solution is essentially important for the inner well-being of man, which, by Divine Providence, or, I ought to say, Divine Justice, rests upon quite other grounds, making it possible, as the Alchemists say, for the poor to be "employed in making the Philosopher's Stone"; that is, the most humble man living may be honest, and enjoy the blessings of probity. Whoever is conscious of a failure on this point is disqualified for passing an adverse judgment upon the *results* claimed as the fruit of well-doing; for the work is one of experience, as all of the writers testify, — in what I understand to be the spirit of the text, John vii. 17: "If any man will do his will, he shall know of the doctrine, whether it be of God or whether I speak of myself." Whoever will rightly interpret this text, and abide by it, will find the "pearl of great price"; and what does it signify whether it be called a pearl, or a stone, the Magaritte of Chaucer's Testament of Love, or the "Rose" of the Romaunt.

It may surprise many to be told that Chaucer was an Alchemist, yet he is claimed and quoted as one by many of the writers. The truth is, he understood Alchemy in the sense that Robert Boyle did, and approved of it; but he saw the errors of false or misled Alchemists, and wrote the *Canon's Tale* to bring them to their senses; but the Tale itself is nevertheless an alchemical work; — as is that of Otto Tachenius, already referred to, written for the same purpose.

The poems of Jean de Meung are all alchemical, including the *Remonstrance of Nature against Wandering Alchemists*, which is not against Alchemy, but against *erring* Alchemists, designed to bring them back to the truth. The Roman de la Rose, begun by William de Lorris, was completed by Jean de Meung, and is itself one of the most complete specimens of Hermetic Philosophy extant. The *Rose* is the symbol of the philosophic gold, and nothing else. The edition of this Romance published at Amsterdam in 1735 is, in fact, a collection of Alchemical Tracts.

As a mere question of literature, there is more in this subject than is generally imagined. There is undoubtedly an unexplored mass of secret writing in existence, which proceeded from men of thought in past ages, especially near the period of the Reformation, which, if it could be deciphered, would throw a great deal of light upon the history of the time and upon the nature of man; but to enter this field fully would require both patience and genius. To examine this subject properly, it would be necessary to look into many works on Magic, Astrology, and Chiromancy, for there was a class of men who wrote on these sciences (?) who were not themselves duped, however much they might have misled others. This has often been suggested; but no one, so far as I know, has undertaken to explore these writings, except from idle curiosity. In the Diary of Elias Ashmole may be seen repeated entries, that he attended the "*Feast* of the Astrologers," without the smallest notice of their proceedings. It is extremely improbable that an association, including such men as Ashmole, were deluded by astrological nonsense, though it is quite possible that under astrological pretensions the wits of the time might have found a freedom denied them in public.

I may be told that, in the same Diary, Ashmole tells us of his curing some distemper by hanging three spiders around his neck. This may or may not have a literal signification. Ashmole was an

Alchemist, and published two collections of alchemical works, besides writing a work on Alchemy himself; which, however, does not rank very high.

It is remarkable that the best works on Alchemy are short, and most of them anonymous. Notwithstanding the unity of doctrine among them, the mode of treatment is so diversified that it is impossible to classify them. Some hold something like a regular order in their treatises; others purposely invert everything, commencing with the end or the middle of the work. Some speak of a *first* work, others of a second, calling it the first, &c.; so that the books at first sight are perfectly chaotic, and one knows not what to make of them. If I had fallen in with them in early life, I should probably have despised them, but meeting with them at a mature age, after I had been sufficiently schooled in the difficulties of what is commonly called Philosophy, I was quite ready to believe that so much labor could hardly have been undertaken without a respectable purpose, by men who manifestly looked for no earthly reward. During the last two years, I have done little else than read these works, and, though I would not recommend any one to follow my example, I do not regret the time I have employed upon this study, even though I have not yet come to a definite conclusion beyond what I have chosen to call *the Way*, about which I am very sure I am not mistaken. *The End* points at some sense of the Unity which I think very few men reach, except in words; for what, indeed, is the real sense involved in the first article of the Creed? Undoubtedly it lies out of the common observation of man, and can only be obtained by a discipline unknown to ordinary teachers. On this point I have no desire to dogmatize, and am willing to leave the subject where I found it, under the rose. The subject cannot be approached with too much gravity, and if I have said a word that may seem to imply any other disposition, I most cheerfully retract it.

In reading books of Alchemy the reader will often find such expressions as these: " herein lies the whole secret"; or, "this is the whole work"; or, "this is all you need"; and the like; but upon comparing what is said in one place as exhibiting the whole work with what is said in another, no likeness will be discovered. This arises from the fact, or what is claimed as such, that the work is "*circular*," and is so concatenated or connected in all its (inseparable) parts that whoever gets a clew to any one of the parts may be said to have found the whole. Hence one writer may say that the whole secret lies in extracting the philosophic mercury, although this is but the base of the work. Another insists that the whole secret lies in making the visible invisible, and the invisible visible. Another may say that the secret lies in dissolution and congelation, which refers to the two extremes of the work, dissolution being considered the unprisoning of the mercury, while congelation or fixation refers to the final indissoluble *union*. Other writers point to the *union* alone as containing the whole secret.

"Our Art," says one, "is to compound two principles, — one in which the Salt, and another in which the Sulphur of Nature doth abound, [the reader may consider that the author is referring to the Sol and Luna of Artephius and others,]—which are not yet perfect, nor altogether imperfect, and by consequence, therefore, may be exalted by our Art, which cannot be effected upon that which is already perfect; and then by common mercury to extract, not the *pondus* [i. e. the substance of the subject], but the celestial virtue out of the compound." The compound is man, and the common mercury is the conscience, by means of which the subject is to be brought under the influence of Divine Love; for "the Love of man for God, and the Love of God for man, is one thing." This "celestial virtue," the author goes on to say, "being *fermental*, begets in the common mercury an offspring more noble than itself, which is our true Hermaphrodite, which will congeal itself."

"Three kinds of most beautiful flowers," says another, "are to be sought, and may be found in the garden of the Wise: damask-colored Violets [love], the milk-white Lily [purity], and the immortal Amaranthus [immortality]. Not far from the fountain, at the entrance, fresh violets do first salute thee, which being watered by streams from the great golden river, put on the most delicate color of the dark sapphire; the sun will give thee signs./ Thou must not sever such precious flowers from their root until thou makest the Stone; for the fresh ones cropped off have more juice and tincture; and then pick them carefully with a gentle and discreet hand; if fates frown not, they will easily follow, and one flower being plucked, the other golden one will not be wanting: let the Lily and the Amaranth succeed with greater care and labor."

This is a synopsis of the whole work.

There are many detached descriptions of the

work pointing more especially to the Unity, passing over or touching but slightly upon the *means* or *the Way*.

Here is one, entitled, —

"A DESCRIPTION OF THE STONE.

"Though *Daphne* fly from *Phœbus* bright,
   Yet shall they both be one,
And if you understand this right,
   You have our hidden stone.
For Daphne, she is fair and white;
   But Volatile is she;
Phœbus a fixed God of might,
   And red as blood is he.
Daphne is a water Nymph,
   And hath of moisture store,
Which Phœbus doth consume with heat,
   And dries her very sore.
They being dried into one,
   Of crystal flood must drink,
Till they be brought to a White Stone;
   Which wash with virgin's milk,
So long until they flow as wax,
   And no fume you can see;
Then have you all you need to ask:
   Praise God, and thankful be."

The "flowing like wax" is the pliability of the subject, become "as a little child." Matt. xviii. 3.

Here is another sample, entitled, —

"ENIGMA PHILOSOPHICUM.

"There is no light but what lives in the Sun;
    There is no Sun but what is twice begot,
Nature and Art the parents first begun;
    By Nature 't was, but Nature perfects not.
        Art then what Nature left in hand doth take,
        And out of one a twofold work doth make.

"A twofold work doth make, but such a work
    As doth admit division, none at all,
(See here wherein the secret most doth lurk,)
    Unless it be a mathematical.
        It must be two; yet make it one and one,
        And you do take the way to make it none.

"Lo here the *Primmer Secret* of this Art:
    Contemn it not, but understand it right;
Who faileth to attain this foremost part,
    Shall never know *Art's force* nor *Nature's might*,
        Nor yet have power of *one* and *one* so mixed,
        To make by *one fixed, one unfixed fixed*."

The above refers entirely to the *End*, and says nothing of the means of attaining it; but, for its purpose, it is one of the most complete descriptions to be found anywhere.

Here is still another, entitled, —

"THOMAS ROBINSON'S DE LAPIDE PHILOSOPHORUM.

"The Heavens, the Earth, and all that in them is,
    Were in six days perfected from abyss:

From one sprung four; from four a second one;
The last a *gritt;* the *First* the corner stone.
Without the *First,* the *last* may not be had;
Yet to the *First,* the *last* is too too bad.
When from the Earth the Heavens were separated,
Were not the Heavens with Earth first cohobated?
And when the Heavens, and Earth, and All were not,
Were only Heavens create, and Earth forgot?
No: Heavens and Earth sprung all from One at first:
Then who can say, or Heavens or Earth is worst?
Is not the Earth the mother of them all?
And what the Heavens, but Earth's essential?
Although they have in Heaven no Earthly residence,
Yet in the Earth doth rest their Heavenly influence:
Were not the Earth, what were the other three?
Were not the Heavens, what on Earth could be?
Thus as they came, so shall they pass together;
But unto man not known from whence, or whither.
And for the time of Earth's Heaven purifying,
Six thousand years they live, and have their dying:
Then all shall rest eternal and divine,
And by the beauty of the Godhead shine.
I swear there is no other truth but this
Of that great *Stone;* which many seek and miss."

The *Marrow of Alchemy,* though the versification is rather of the doggerel order, contains many useful directions, of which I will give the following as a specimen:—

"Consider well the danger, and be sure
That better 't is in safety than in fear

To live, and so you shall yourself inure
To secrecy, that none from you may hear,
 Either in boasting way, what you can do,
 Nor yet for price procure the secret true."

The danger here referred to was that of persecution for opinion's sake, to guard against which secrecy is recommended.

"Of drink and eke of company beware,
The one besots, the other eke allures:
Secret he cannot be, to drink that dare
Too largely; Temperance best assures:
 This is the Bar that doth command the tongue,
 Without which can it not be bridled long.

"All these things ordered right, next I advise
Thee not t' expect with over-greedy mind
The event, but mind the sayings of the wise,
By patience long, the end you sure will find;
 He that hopes in short time to receive
 His harvest, doth himself in fine deceive.

"Some cannot let their glass stand quiet long,
But they it move, or turn, or jog, or shake;
Thereby they do to Nature's work much wrong,
Which forced is her own Path to forsake,
 And follow these fond Artists' foolish mind;
 Which whoso violates, may reap the wind.

"Commit thyself, and work, to God above;
Intreat his grace, and help, and from all sin
And vice thee keep, which God's laws do reprove;
With Him alone see that thou do begin,

This is the way success for to attain,
Else may'st thou toil, but always toil in vain.

"And if thou hap so blessed for to be,
As this rare Jewel to attain, which many
Do miss, few find, be sure in thy degree
That God thou honor; neither do to any
Wrong in the least, for so to God thou wilt
Obnoxious be under a heinous guilt.

"The poor relieve, the sick from danger free;
In napkin bury not this talent great;
Charitable works pursue; so shalt thou see
God's blessing on thee resting, and on thy seat,
Whilst thou with mortals haste; yet O resolve
With God at last to live; this oft revolve:

"For this of all the blessings of this life
The greatest is, and of the highest price;
Nor is it given but to such, whose strife
Is to improve it; such who (truly wise)
Do not so doat on that which fading is,
As to neglect the everlasting bliss.

"Now shall I briefly, plainly, and indeed,
The real workings of our Stone disclose,
With all its colors, and its days: my rede
Whoso observes, shall find it truly shows
More than by any man hath been revealed,
And yet there's something herein lies concealed.

"The Fire thy compound shall no sooner feel,
But altogether like to lead will flow;
The tender Body, which the soul of steel
Is, doth such mighty efficacy show,

That Sol is whitened, and in it devoured;
On both *Medea's* broth must then be poured.

" This is our Sea, in which Two Fishes swim,
Yet neither Fish hath either scale or bone;
The Sea is ever round, yet hath no brim,
The *Sea* and *Fishes* eke are all, but *One;*
   These we digest until a broth they make,
   That all may in the Unity partake.

" Attend thou forty days; then shall appear
Black of the blackest, like a well-burnt coal;
When this thou seest, thou shalt not need to fear,
But White at last shall show without control;
   And so unto the sparkling Red you come,
   Having at first of Blackness passed the doom.

" Thus Blackness is the gate by which we enter
To Light of Paradise; this is the way;
The Bodies here reduced are, to their center:
A dismal night brings forth a glorious day.
   Let this thy study be, this Black t' attain,
   Or else all other signs shall be in vain.

" The color first is Argent, for the Sun
In the womb of Luna must descend,
And both unto their Matter First must run,
By *Mercury* alone, which doth amend
   Nature in its kind, that Sun and Moon
   Are both eclipsed in this *Water* soon.

" The Fire still working is the only cause
Of all this alteration which doth

>   Appear; by means of this the Water draws
>   Water of Life from Sun and Luna both:
>   This Water hides a *Spirit* of great might,
>   The proper seed of *Sol* and *Luna* bright."

I will follow this no further, for here, as in other extracts, my object is not to attempt a complete exhibition of the " Great Work," but to show that the Alchemists were students of *man,* and to justify the hint of Dr. Kopp, that, if it be allowed to consider man as a microcosm, the interpretation of the writings of the Alchemists will be " easy "; for this is his judgment upon the very extracts cited by the French writer, and copied by the English Reviewer, to show how absurdly the Alchemists went to work to make gold.

Alchemy has passed away, the Reviewer says, never to return; and this may be so: but the questions about which the Alchemists employed themselves have not passed away, and never shall pass away while man wanders upon the surface of the earth. They are the most interesting questions which the heart can propose, and although they begin in man, the answer must compass both the microcosm and macrocosm; and their prosecution is attended at this day with the same difficulties and dangers that have always surrounded them, making it uncertain whether those who think they have attained the truth are at liberty to publish it, lest the vain and frivolous should fancy themselves wise by learning to repeat by rote dogmas beyond their comprehension; for the couplet of Pope is true,

"Drink deep, or taste not," &c.

The warnings of Espagnet are worthy of all consideration.

"Whosoever is disposed to seek the Philosopher's Stone, let him resolve to make a long journey, for it is necessary that he see both the Indies," i. e: he must examine and understand the extreme boundaries of nature, as defined and terminated by active and passive; spirit and matter; soul and body; Sol and Luna; Daphne and Phœbus; Heaven and Earth; the two doves of Diana; the two Fishes of the Sea without brim; and must discover the mediating principle by which all contraries are reconciled; to do which he must understand the nature of the fixed and the volatile, in order — as Espagnet proceeds — "that from thence he may bring the most precious gems and the purest gold."

"Whoever affirmeth that the Philosopher's Grand Secret is above the strength of nature and art, is blind; because he knows not the *Sun* and *Moon*."

"Metals, we must confess, cannot be perfected by the instinct and labor of Nature only (1 Cor. ii. 14); yet we may affirm that the perfecting virtue is hid in their profundity, and manifesteth itself by the help of Art. In this work Nature standeth in need of the aid of Art; and both doth perfect the whole."

"Let those who are desirous of a knowledge of Chemistry [Alchemy], and have hitherto followed impostors and mountebanks, sound a retreat, spare time and cost, and give their minds to a work truly philosophical, lest the *Phrygians* be wise too late, and at length be compelled to cry out with the prophet, *Strangers have eaten up my strength.*"

"In the Philosopher's work, more toil and time than cost is expended; for he that hath convenient matter need be at little expense: besides, those that hunt after great store of money, and place their chief end in wealth, trust more to their riches than to their own Art. Let, therefore, the too credulous freshman beware of those pilfering pickpockets that lay in wait for gold; they demand bright ushering *Sol*, because they walk in darkness."

"As those that sail between *Scylla* and *Charybdis* are in danger on both sides, unto no less hazard are they subject who, pursuing the prey of the golden fleece, are carried between the uncertain rocks of the Philosopher's *Sulphur* and *Mercury*. The more acute, by their constant reading of grave and credible authors, and by the irradiant *Sun*, have attained unto the knowledge of *Sulphur*, but are at a stand in the entrance of the Philosopher's *Mercury;* for writers have twisted it with so many windings and meanders, and involved it with so many equivocal names, that it may be sooner met with by the force of the *Seeker's Intellect*, than be found by reason or toil."

The "Sun" here spoken of is the same *Sun* that illuminated the *two* precious jewels at the bottom of the well in the *Romaunt of the Rose*, for that poem, as I have already said, is a perfect specimen of Hermetic Philosophy, mistaken as it commonly is for a *love-tale*.

"Nature proceedeth thus in making and perfecting her works," (I still have Espagnet before me,) "that from an inchoate generation it may bring a thing by diverse means, as it were by degrees, to the ultimate term of perfection. She therefore attaineth her end by little and little, and not by leaps, confining and including her work between two extremes, distinct and severed as by spaces. The practice of Philosophy, which is the ape of Nature, ought not to decline from the way and example of Nature in its working and direction to find out its happy Stone; for whosoever is without the bounds of Nature is either in error, or nearest one."

"The whole progress of the Philosopher's work is nothing but *solution* and *congelation* [dishearten a man first, and then encourage and fortify him, but according to the laws of his own nature, and without violence], — the solution of the body, and the congelation of the spirit; nevertheless, there is but one operation of both: the fixed and volatile are perfectly mixed and united in the spirit, which cannot be done unless the fixed body be first made soluble and volatile. By reduction is the volatile body fixed into a permanent body, and volatile nature doth at last change into a fixed one, as the fixed nature had before passed into a volatile one. Now, so long as the natures were confused in the spirit, that mixed spirit keeps a middle nature between body and spirit, fixed and volatile."

"The generation of the Stone is made after the pattern of the creation of the world; for it is necessary that it have its chaos and first matter, wherein the confused elements do fluctuate, until they be separated by the Fiery Spirit: they being separated, the light elements are carried upwards, and the heavy ones downwards. The Light arising, the Darkness retreats: the waters are gathered into one, and the dry land appears. At length the *Two Great Luminaries* arise, and mineral virtues, vegetable and animal, are produced in the Philosopher's Earth [in the Man]."

"The Elixir's perfection consisteth in the strict union and indissoluble matrimony of *Siccum* and *Humidum* [of Phœbus and Daphne], so that they may not be separated, but the *Siccum* may flow with moderate heat into the *Humidum*, abiding every pressure of the Fire. [James i. 12.]

"A Three-headed Dragon keeps the Golden Fleece. The First Head proceedeth from the Waters; the Second, from the Earth; the Third, from the Air. It is necessary that these Three Heads do end in One most Potent, which shall devour all the other Dragons: then a way is laid open for thee to the Golden Fleece.

"Farewell, diligent reader. In reading these things, invocate the Spirit of Eternal Light; speak little, meditate much, and judge aright."

And this is good advice, whether the Truth be sought in one direction or another.

As the union of *Sol* and *Luna* is so much insisted on by these writers, I will adduce another example of it from an Alchemist of considerable authority, or rather distinction; for we must not forget that mere authority is of but little importance with this class of students, with whom the Truth alone is the sovereign authority.

" Now, that you may avoid false processes, and have a sure foundation to build upon, as to particulars, so as to make them profitable, and fail neither in the beginning, continuation, nor end of your Work, I shall lay down the following *Philosophic verity*, for a Rule, viz.: —

" *You must unite Sol and Luna* [here are the *two fishes* in Medea's broth, *Phœbus* and *Daphne*, *Siccum* and *Humidum*, etc., etc., etc., etc.] *so firmly and absolutely, that they may be for ever inseparable.* [The reader, surely, need not be told that this is not a work of the hands.] If you know not how to do this, you know nothing truly in our Art.

" Understand this thing rightly, and lay hold of it with diligence, so will the veil of Ignorance be taken from your eyes; for all processes which centre not in this verity are vain and false.

" Now, that you may have no cause to complain of the brevity of the afore-declared *philosophic verity*, hear further what the Ancients and great men in this Art say:— *You must so join or mix gold and silver* [Sol and Luna again] *that they may not, by any possible means whatever, be separated.*

"What think you, if I should so perfectly unite these two Bodies,— what would this Union come to ? The Searcher after Truth must judge. TRY.

"But truly I tell thee, that this united *Sol* and *Luna*, if perfectly effected, can never be separated; no, neither by *Aqua fortis*, nor by any other *trial* whatever.

"And when they are thus united, it is a very great and profitable particular: for here *Luna*, by the virtue and power of *Sol*, is totally *fixed*, graduated, and made ponderous.

"This is the particular which the Ancients, learned in this *Art*, bid you to understand; that you may be able to proceed on to the conclusion of the great Work.

"Here *Luna* rides on a chariot of four wheels, like *Sol*, viz. *color, fixity, malleability*, and *ponderosity*. Here she borrows six measures of the Sun, and as a Queen, wears the King's Crown. Here the Frigidity is conquered by the Calidity; and the White Woman becomes the Red Man.

"And here the true *Filius Hermetis* may see, that

the doctrine of the true Philosophers differs much from the juggling processes of the deceivers, *for that our particulars have their offspring from the Root of the true universal subject.*

"And it is the greatest of Truths, *that the conjunction and union of the Bodies of Sol and Luna is the real beginning of our true medicine, elixir, or tincture.*

"Among the vulgar processes there is nothing but falsehood and deceit, wherein the *Luna* is never *fixed*, but is wanting in ponderosity, and black; having been only washed, and fixed (as they call it) with Salt, and graduated with the Sulphurs of *Mars* and *Venus*, and made ponderous with *Saturn*.

"O foolishness! O blindness of mind! can common Salt be the Soap [another name for the water of Hollandus, the vinegar of Artephius, &c.] of the Philosopher? Can common Saturn, or its vitrum, ever become *our* ponderous *Ruby Star, our Red Fixed Eagle, our Red Fixed Sulphur of Sol*, or *our Fixed Salamander*, ever living in the Fire?

"He that hath once truly obtained the right *Augmentum*, is assured that he has met with the infallible verity, with an incorruptible Tincture, yea, with an infinite Treasure; and needs the help of no other Instructor.

"This Augmentum in the particular and universal way, is to be kept in the profundity of Philosophic Silence; and when discoursed of, to be done only in parables, riddles, and similitudes, and as it were at a distance, that profane and vile persons may be kept from the knowledge thereof.

"The possessor of this Treasure has no occasion to run to kings, princes, lords, nobles, or great men; they who do so have none of the Secret, but desire to try conclusions at other men's charges.

"The true possessor seeks not after such friendships, or earthly glories: he is content with his *modicum*, or little, and has enough, even the whole world in his Philosopher's egg, which he can carry about with him wherever he goes."

If the reader can discover what the two Bodies truly are, which are so constantly referred to by these writers, he will make a great step towards understanding their theory. But he must not imagine he knows them by any mere *names* whatever, for these vary indefinitely under a constantly prevailing idea. In the Sophist of Plato the idea may be sought, perhaps successfully, in the discussion upon the words *entity* and *nonentity*, the student carefully noticing how *entity* is made to disappear, and how *nonentity* is brought in among things that *are*, the difficulty of understanding either being very fully illustrated and insisted on.

It may also greatly assist to read Cratylus some half a dozen times, under the idea that it is a symbolical discussion upon the nature of *things* under the form of an inquiry about *names*. "What is this very thing, *name?*" that is, what is a *thing?* The "name-founder" is God.

In reality, the question of the Trinity in Unity is involved in this subject; to wit, in what sense two (somethings) can be conceived as one, which, with the two, constitute a Trinity in Unity. It is a considerable step towards satisfaction, when the student is impressed with the notion that the Truth, whatever it be, is irrevocable and irreversible; and that 't is our business to discover it, if possible; not to change it, or to influence it in any manner, but to accommodate ourselves to it.

In the Sanscrit *Bhagvat Geeta*, translated by Wilford, it is declared to be the height of wisdom to perceive *action in inaction*, and *inaction in action;* which means, if it means anything, that cause (active) and effect (passive) are two modes of the manifestation of one thing. In harmony with this construction, Plato says in the Philebus, that causes, taken universally, and effects, taken universally, are one and the same; for, in the nature of things, every particular cause of something must itself be the particular effect of something; and so, in like manner, every particular effect becomes a cause, or, more strictly speaking, the *occasion* or *condition* under which the uncaused existence in itself acts within itself.

But there is need, says Plato, in the Parmenides, of a person naturally clever to discover these things, and of a person still more wonderful to be able to explain them in a sufficiently clear manner.

The Alchemists all refer the student to God, the uncaused cause of all things, who alone commands, Let there be Light; — and they tell us that the mere study of books cannot attain to it; which is, no doubt, one reason among others for their mystical mode of writing of *Salt*, *Sulphur*, and *Mercury*. They say it can only be learned by inspiration, or by the teaching of one who has so learned it; but yet it should be stated, that they consider a sound understanding as the gift of God; — and he certainly must, of all men, be the most blind, who denies that his faculties are gifts of the Most High.

I feel that I shall not have accomplished my purpose, if I omit to notice the History of the Alchemists, published by Charles Mackay, LL. D., included in a couple of volumes (1852) entitled, *Memoirs of Extraordinary Popular Delusions, and the Madness of Crowds.* Dr. Mackay has devoted some hundred and thirty pages of close print, duodecimo, to the Alchemists, and has given sketches, or what purport to be such, of some forty *Searchers for the Philosopher's Stone, and the Water of Life.*

In the whole of this work I do not observe a single paragraph to show that Dr. Mackay took any other than the most literal view of the *Work* of the class of men whose memoirs he assumed to write. He seems not to have had the slightest suspicion that the Hermetic Philosophers had any other object in their studies and labors than gold, or the discovery of an agent for lengthening life. He nowhere shows that the improvement, not to say perfection of life, can ever have been an object with them, but has brought together all sorts of ridiculous stories, most of which carry their refutation on their face, while many of the extracts he has given from the writings of the Alchemists are of such a character as to suggest, one would think, a double sense, even to the most ordinary reader.

Many of those peculiar men, according to Dr. Mackay's own account, sacrificed ease, honors, and wealth, and submitted even to the loss of life, in pursuit of one absorbing object; and yet he nowhere shows the slightest capacity for discovering the nature of that object.

When I first saw these Memoirs, my curiosity, chiefly, was awakened, and I searched the volume to discover the real object of the Alchemists, hoping that it might indirectly appear, for it was plain that the author knew nothing of it; but I cared very little about the volume otherwise. Now, however, this History strikes me as one of the saddest books I have ever had in my hands. Here is an entire class of men, scattered through many centuries, devoting their whole lives to the highest objects that can engage the attention of man, — to the study of wisdom, the knowledge of God, and the nature of the human soul, — and yet, almost without exception, they are represented as a parcel of fools, vagabonds, and impostors! Though some of them are admitted by the author of this History to have possessed the highest genius, he was incapable of even surmising a hidden purpose in all their industrious "folly" in pursuit of the Philosopher's Stone, but with the greatest pains he has labored to consign their memory to the contempt of all after ages.

That some of the individuals whose lives (?) have been written by Dr. Mackay were impostors, I willingly concede, as freely as I confess that multitudes of men have led the lives of wolves under the mask of following the Lamb of God; but where is the excuse for one who formally attempts to instruct the world by an historical memoir, without information as a foundation, and without the ability to discriminate between the true and the false, and most likely, in this case, without even consulting the writings of the men of whom he assumed to write the history, where, at least, he would have found the most abundant warnings not to understand them literally?

"The philosophers," says one, "ever discourse in parables and figures; nor is it fit that all things should be revealed to everybody: the matter is to be inquired after, and diligently searched into; — without labor and pains, nothing is to be obtained; but wisdom enters not into profane souls, nor dwells in a body subject to sin, as the wise man affirms."

"Let the studious reader," says another, "have a care of the manifold signification of words, for by deceitful windings, and doubtful, yea, contrary speeches, (as it should seem,) philosophers unfold their mysteries, with a desire of concealing and hiding the truth from the unworthy, not of sophisticating or destroying it."

Flammel illustrated the subject with hieroglyphic figures, which he explained at length, but still in cipher. In one place he refers to "the Three Persons rising again, clothed in sparkling white, which represent," says he, "the *Body, Soul,* and *Spirit* of our White Stone."

"The philosophers," says he, "do commonly use these terms to hide the secret from unworthy men. They call the Body that *Black Earth*, which is obscure and dark, and which we make white. They call the *Soul* the other half, divided from the body, which, by the purpose of God, and work of nature, gives to the Body, by its Imbibitions and Fermentations, a *vegetable* Soul; viz. a Power and Virtue to bud, or spring, increase, multiply, and become *white*, like a naked, shining sword.

"They call the Spirit the Tincture and Dryness; which, as a spirit, has power to pierce all things.

"It would be too tedious to tell you how great reason the philosophers had to say always, and in all places, *Our Stone hath, answerable to human kind, a Body, a Soul, and a Spirit.*

"I will only inculcate to you, that as a man endued with *Body, Soul,* and *Spirit* is, notwithstanding, one man, or substance; so likewise in this your *White Compositum*, you have but one only substance, yet containing a *Body, Soul*, and *Spirit*, which are inseparably united.

"I could easily give you most clear comparisons and expositions of this *Body, Soul*, and *Spirit*, not fit to be divulged; but should I explicate them, I must, of necessity, declare things which God reserves to Himself, to reveal to a select few of such as fear and love him, and therefore ought not to be written."

"Let me entreat you," says Combachius, in his *Epistle to the Reader*, "to take notice, that when you find any mention made of *heaven, earth, soul, spirits*, or *our heaven*, &c., these are not meant the *celestial heaven*, or *natural earth*, but terms used by the philosophers to obscure their sayings from the wicked; spoken with all due and holy reverence to the *Divine* Majesty."

"I would have the courteous Reader be here admonished," says Sandivogius, "that he understand my writings, not so much from the outside of my words, as from the possibility of nature; lest afterwards he bewail his time, pains, and costs, all spent in vain. Let him consider that this Art is for the wise, not for the ignorant," &c.

There is scarcely a single writer upon this *Art*, who does not give similar warnings to guard against being understood *literally*. Their writings therefore are nothing but *suggestions* giving occasion for thought in the reader, who must look into himself and into nature for an interpretation.

To refute all of the absurdities to be found in Dr. Mackay's book would greatly exceed my limits. I have already shown with sufficient clearness, except to those who will not or cannot see, that some of the genuine Alchemists, confessed to be such by Dr. Mackay himself, were not in pursuit of either gold or a long life, but simply of a good life; as, Geber, Artephius, Basil Valentine, and some others not named by him, as Hollandus and Van Suchten; and by these examples, though but a few, have sufficiently proved that the so-called *Memoirs* must be worthless, as indeed they are, except to feed the gaping stupidity of fools.

Dr. Mackay, after telling us that Peter Aponus was an "eminent physician," closes the sad story of this martyr with didactic coldness, and without one syllable of sympathy, in these words: —

"Having given utterance to some sentiments regarding religion which were the very reverse of orthodox, he was summoned before the tribunal of the Inquisition to answer for his crimes as a heretic and a sorcerer. He loudly protested his innocence, even upon the rack, where he suffered more torture than nature could support. He died in prison ere his trial was concluded, but was afterwards found guilty. His bones were ordered to be dug up and publicly burned. He was also burned in effigy in the streets of Padua."

It may seem hardly charitable to say so, but one may almost think that the writer of this account would have assisted in the proceedings he so coldly records, had he been present, and never once have thought that the guiding spirit of those horrible abominations was the very same that presided in the dreadful scene enacted in Jerusalem in the reign of Tiberius.

Peter Aponus, the Alchemist, would have done better to have kept his speech within the charmed language of the class of men with whom he held sympathy. He might then freely have talked of Salt, Sulphur, and Mercury, and would have escaped the persecution and tyranny of the most abominable of all tribunals that ever disgraced the world.

The reader, in view of this account of an "eminent physician," is requested to bear in mind one of the reasons I have assigned for the esoteric writing of the Hermetic Philosophers. In the age of Aponus, 1250, Luther himself would have been burned at the stake; but by such men as Aponus the way had been prepared for the great Reformer, who merely proclaimed doctrines, the seeds of which had been sown some centuries in advance of his appearance in the world. It was by the labors of such men as Peter Aponus in the eleventh, twelfth, thirteenth, and fourteenth centuries, that Europe was sufficiently indoctrinated in the principles of free inquiry to make it comparatively safe to speak openly, as Luther did. The result, in our day, is perfect freedom of speech and writing, except from the low and vulgar tyranny of popular opinion; and it is the duty of all who know how to prize the privileges of independence, to do justice to those who prepared the way for it.

One of the finest philosophic wits of his time, an Alchemist, was Bernard of Treves, sometimes called Trevisan, and often the *good* Trevisan. "He was born at Treves or Padua," says Mackay, "in the year 1406." Dr. Mackay introduces him to his readers in these words:—

"The life of this philosopher is a remarkable instance of talent and perseverance misapplied. In the search of his chimera, nothing could daunt him. Repeated disappointment never diminished his hopes; and from the age of fourteen to that of eighty-five he was incessantly employed among *the drugs and furnaces of his laboratory*, wasting his life with a view of prolonging it, and reducing himself to beggary in the hopes of growing rich."

If Dr. Mackay had simply said that Bernard employed the whole of a long life in the pursuit and practice of truth and goodness, he would have summed up all that need be said of him; — except to give some account of his works, instead of which the historian has occupied several pages in recording a series of absurd stories, not one of which can possibly have been true of the man who wrote the *Letter to Thomas of Bononia*, where Bernard treats of Alchemy. In order to be sure of this, it is only necessary to know something of Alchemy and of the *style* of writing about it, and then to read the *Letter* with some, even faint, shadow of the critical spirit of Niebuhr. The author of the Letter never was guilty of the follies attributed to him.

I will make a short extract from this Letter, by which any one may see that Bernard was of a spirit kindred to that of Artephius, Valentine, and others, who wrote of Truth symbolically, when it was dangerous to speak openly.

The reader will please remember the principles of Artephius, and observe the parallel.

"He therefore that knows the art and secret of *dissolution*, hath attained the secret point of the art, which is to mingle thoroughly the *natures*, and out of natures [he means, of the Soul and Body] to extract natures which are effectually hid in them." The reader must bear in mind the doctrine of Hollandus and others, that *Saturn* is gold internally; that is, that man contains a seed of goodness and truth within him, and the only point is to bring it out and make it active without destroying the subject of it. For this purpose *dissolution* is here declared to be necessary, which means that the man must by gentle means, naturally, and not violently, be made modest and humble; or, in short, must be brought into the state of simplicity and truthfulness which Christ declared essential in him who would enter the kingdom of heaven. Bernard next proceeds to oppose the practice of those who use violent means for this object, and says:—" How then can it be said that he hath found the truth, who destroys the moist nature of Quicksilver? [By Quicksilver here, we are to understand the *water* of Hollandus and the *antimonial vinegar* of Artephius, i. e. the conscience:] as those fools who deform its nature from its metallic [heavenly] disposition, and, dissolving its radical moisture, corrupt it, and thus disproportion *Quicksilver* from its first mineral quality, — which needs nothing but purity and simple decoction."

The point in this doctrine, and, as I have said repeatedly, it is the essential *starting-point* in Hermetic discipline (or philosophy), is, not to act upon the conscience through any of the passions, hope, fear, or any other passion, to improve man; but, as far as possible, allay these or neutralize them, so as to open the way for the conscience to act freely, and according to its own essential, heavenly nature; and this, then, according to Pontanus, "will do the whole work, without any laying on of hands." Bernard proceeds to enforce his view: —

"For example: — they who defile it with salts, vitriols, and aluminous things, do destroy it, and change it into some other thing than is the nature of *Quicksilver*. For that *seed* which Nature by its sagacity composed, they endeavor to perfect by violence, which undoubtedly is destructive to it, so far as it is useful and effective in *our Work*......
For example: — Fools draw corrosive waters from inferior minerals [pernicious doctrines from inferior teachers], into which they cast the species of metals,

and corrode them: for they think that they are thereby dissolved with a natural solution; but this solution, to be permanent, requires a permanency of the *dissolver and the dissolved*, that a new Seed may result from both the masculine and feminine seed [i. e. the Soul and Body, naturally dissolved by the conscience, which belongs to them, and remains with them, are prepared for a new birth 'in the air,' that is, the Spirit]. I tell you assuredly," continues Bernard, "that no *Water* dissolves any metallic species by a *natural Solution*, save that which abides with them in matter and form, and which the metals themselves, being dissolved, can recongeal; which happens not when *Aquaforts* are used, which do rather defile the compound, that is, the Body [i. e. the man] to be dissolved; neither is that water proper for solutions, which abides not with them in their coagulations, and finally *Mercury* is of this sort, and not *Aquaforts;* nor that which fools imagine to be a limpid and diaphanous mercurial water: for if they divide or abstract the homogeneity of *Mercury*, how can the first proportion of the feminine seed consist and be preserved? Because *Mercury* cannot receive congelation with the dissolved Bodies, neither will the true nature be renovated afterwards in the administration of the *Art;* nay, but some other filthy and unprofitable thing."

I am strongly tempted to explain a point here hinted at, but I will leave it to be discovered by those who have observed the temporary effects of mere excitement and enthusiasm.

"Yet thus they think they dissolve, mistaking nature, but dissolve not: for *aquaforts* being abstracted, or taken away, [the external causes of excitement being removed,] the Body becometh *meltable* as before, and that water abides not with, nor subsists in, the Body, as its radical moisture. The Bodies indeed are corroded, but not dissolved; and by how much more they are corroded, they are so much the more estranged from a true metallic [heavenly] nature."

The *Bodies* that are here spoken of are the two constituents of man, called the Soul and Body, commonly supposed to be well known by their mere names. These in what, for convenience, is called their natural state, — not that, strictly speaking, there is or can be an unnatural state, — are supposed to be at feud with each other (Romans vii. 2, 3,) and in order to their being brought into unity, amity, peace, and concord, the doctrine requires that the man, the "compound," shall be first *dissolved*, that is, humiliated and brought into the state required in Scripture (the man must become as a little child); but this must be done naturally, and by an agent that comes from the compound, and after action abides naturally in it. This agent is the conscience, and no other element of man, such as his passions, his hopes, or his fears, for these are called *aquaforts* and *corrosives*, and are said to destroy the composition instead of perfecting it; and they do not abide with it, but may fly away and leave a "filthy and unprofitable thing," instead of an improved or perfected man.

This is the doctrine, right or wrong, true or false, for I am only stating, not defending it; and this is the foundation of Hermetic Philosophy; but, as I must continue to interpose, not *the End* of it.

Bernard is here enforcing upon his friend, Thomas of Bononia, "physician to King Charles the Eighth," the point that all violent action upon man with a view to his improvement is injurious, and this is the doctrine of Plato: not but that the safety of society may require the use of violent means to restrain criminals who disturb its peace, but in this case the subjects of such action are unfit for the *Work* which the philosophic humanitarian aims at. So, when a man is humbled through his pride, and cannot say with Julius in Measure for Measure, " I do repent me as it is an evil, and take the shame with joy," or when he is arrested by external disappointments, he is not in a proper state to fulfil the condition required by philosophy for natural and permanent improvement, but he is driven violently out of the true channel for it.

"These solutions, therefore," continues Bernard, "are not the foundation of the *Art of Transmutation*, but they are rather the impostures of sophistical Alchemists [false or ignorant teachers, the erring Alchemists addressed by Jean de Meung in his *Remonstrance*], who think that this sacred Art is hid in them. They say, indeed, that they make solutions; but they cannot make perfect *metallic species*, because they do not naturally remain under the first proportion or nature which *Mercury*, the water, allows in metallic species. For *Mercury* should be corrupted [in the sense of John xii. 24] by way of alteration, not dissipation; because Bodies dissolved therein are never separated from it, as in *Aquafortis* and other *corrosives*, but one nature puts on and hides another, retaining it secretly and perfectly: so, Sol and Luna dissolved, are secretly retained in it. For their nature is hid in Mercury, even unto its condensation, of which they lying hid in it are the cause, inasmuch as they are latent in it: and as Mercury dissolves them, and hides them in its Belly, so they also congeal it; and what was hard is made soft, what was soft, hard [it is the property of the conscience to subdue the strong and strengthen the weak]: and yet the nature, that is, metals and *Quicksilver* abide still. . . . . . So the Lord in the Gospel speaks by way of similitude of vegetables, *Unless a grain of corn fallen on earth do die, it abides alone; but if it die, it brings forth much fruit.* Therefore this alterative corruption hides forms, perfects natures, preserves proportions, and changes colors [passions] from the beginning to the end."

If the reader has duly weighed and understood the method described by Artephius and others, in the preceding pages, he cannot fail to see the drift of this doctrine of Bernard, and that the subject of all these writers is one, to wit, man, and the object is also one, to wit, his improvement, while the method is no less one, to wit, nature, directed by art acquired in the school of nature, and acting in conformity with it; for true art is nothing but " nature acting through man."

But here, as everywhere, I am anxious to impress upon the reader that this, so far, is but the beginning or "base" of the "Great Work." When the man is by a due process and without violence brought into a Unity with himself, so that his intellect and will work in harmony, he is prepared to understand that higher Unity which is the perfection of the whole of nature; for what is called the "absolute," the "absolute perfection," and the perfection of nature, are one and the same; which can never be understood except by a process in nature itself proper to it. In no case is there any violation of nature, and, as these writers are perpetually repeating, "men do not gather grapes of thorns, or figs of thistles."

The whole of this epistle of Bernard is a grave discussion upon the nature of man, and yet it is all carried on in the symbolic language, no doubt perfectly understood by the adepts of the time, when those who used the language had opportunities of personal intercourse in which full explanations could be made without interruption from the Inquisition or its emissaries.

Occasionally some of the philosophers, and I take it not the best of them, carried away not precisely by philosophy (i. e. reason), but by a passion or enthusiasm for it, spoke too openly, and brought themselves into danger, and many fell victims to the most relentless spirit that ever disturbed the world.

Let any one, with the above explanations, read the epistle of Bernard of Treves, the "good Trevisan," and then turn to that farrago of nonsensical stories collected by the misemployed industry of Dr. Mackay, LL. D., as "Memoirs" of a man who spent his whole life in the pursuit of truth and goodness, and he must be struck with the absurd position of the historian.

Dr. Mackay undertook to write "Memoirs of Extraordinary Popular Delusions." I would recommend that, before publishing another edition of his work, he would endeavor to understand the delusion of almost the whole world in regard to the object of the Alchemists, in which he himself has shared. The Alchemists themselves were under no delusion, but were the philosophers of the world when philosophy could not speak openly.

To show the necessity of *esoteric* writing we need only look at the fate of Vanini, and Bruno, and thousands of others, burned at the stake, or otherwise cruelly destroyed, by the ignorant priesthood of the time; and why? because

"Out of their heart's fulness they needs must gabble,
And show their thoughts and feelings to the rabble."
(*Brooks, translation of Faust.*)

Of Vanini, Gorton says:—

"Being *suspected* of inculcating atheistical opinions, he was denounced, prosecuted, and condemned to have his tongue cut out, and to be burnt to death, which sentence was executed February 19, 1619. At his trial, so far from denying the existence of God, he took up a straw, and said, that it obliged him to acknowledge the existence of one. Gramont, President of the Parliament of Toulouse, gives an evidently prejudiced and sophisticated account of his deportment at his death, where it seems that, on refusing to put out his tongue for the executioner to cut it off, it was torn from his mouth with pincers, such being the Christianity of the French District, which afterwards got up the tragedy of *Calas*. He suffered this cruel punishment in the thirty-fourth year of his age. Mosheim remarks that several learned and respectable writers regard this unhappy man rather as the victim of bigotry and prejudice than as a martyr to impiety and atheism, and deny that his writings were so absurd or so impious as they were said to be."

Jordano Bruno was burnt at the stake at Venice in the year 1600. After his arrest he was allowed " eighty days," says history, " to retract his errors," but refused to deny his opinions, and suffered the fate which Galileo escaped by admitting that the world stood still, — which he might have said with a clear conscience of the clerical world of his day, for they would neither advance themselves, nor were they disposed to allow others to do so.

Bruno addressed one of his works to Lord Castelnau, then minister from the French government at the court of England, in which he says: —

"If I had held the plough, most illustrious Lord, or fed a flock, or cultivated a garden, or mended old clothes, none would distinguish and few would regard me; fewer yet would reprehend me, and I might easily become agreeable to everybody. But now, for describing the Field of Nature; for being solicitous about the posture of the Soul; for being curious about the improvement of the understanding, and for showing some skill about the faculties of the mind: one man, as if I had an eye to him, does menace me; another, for being only observed, does assault me; for coming near this man, he bites me; and for laying hold of that other, he devours me. 'T is not one who treats me in this manner, nor are they a few; they are many, and almost all.

"If you would know whence this doth proceed, my Lord, the true reason is, that I am displeased with the bulk of mankind; I hate the vulgar rout;

I despise the authority of the multitude, and am enamored with one particular Lady. 'T is for her that I am free in servitude, content in pain, rich in necessity, and alive in death; and therefore 't is likewise for her that I envy not those who are slaves in the midst of liberty, who suffer pain in their enjoyment of pleasure, who are poor though overflowing with riches, and dead when they are reputed to live: for in their body they have the chain that pinches them, and in their judgment the lethargy that kills them; having neither generosity to undertake, nor perseverance to succeed, nor splendor to illustrate their names. Hence it is, even for my passion for this Beauty, that, as being weary, I draw not back my feet from the difficult road, nor, as being lazy, hang down my hands from the work that is before me; I turn not my shoulders, as grown desperate, to the enemy that contends with me; nor, as dazzled, divert my eyes from the divine object.

"In the mean time I know myself to be for the most part accounted a Sophister, more desirous to appear subtle, than to be really solid; an ambitious fellow, that studies rather to set up a new and false sect, than to confirm the ancient and true doctrine; a deceiver, that aims at purchasing brightness to his own fame, by engaging others in the darkness of error; a restless spirit, that overturns the edifice of sound discipline, and makes himself a founder of some hut of perversity.

"But, my Lord, so may all the holy deities deliver me from those that unjustly hate me; so may my own God be ever propitious to me; so may the governors of this our globe show me their favor; so may the stars furnish me with such a seed for the field, and such a field for the seed, that the world may reap the useful and glorious fruit of my labor, by awakening the genius and opening the understanding of such as are deprived of *sight:* so may all these things happen, I say, as it is most certain that I neither feign nor pretend. If I err, I am far from thinking that I do so; and whether I speak or write, I dispute not for the love of victory (for I look upon all reputation and conquest to be hateful to God, — to be most vile and dishonorable, — without *Truth*); but, 't is for the love of true WISDOM, and by the studious admiration of this mistress, that I fatigue, that I disquiet, that I torment myself."

This is the spirit which the Inquisition and the power of all the governments in Europe was employed for many centuries in endeavoring to suppress; and is it surprising that it should force into existence secret societies and mysterious modes of intercourse among those who, like Eyrenæus (Cosmopolita), were, as he says, "tossed up and down, and, as it were, beset with *furies;* nor can we," says he, "suppose ourselves safe in any one place long. We travel through many countries just like vagabonds. Once I was forced to fly by night, with exceeding great trouble, having changed my garments, shaved my head, put on false hair, and altered my name, else I had fallen into the hands of wicked men that lay in wait for me,"— merely, he tells us, because a "*rumor* had spread" that he was in possession of the *Elixir;* — which meant, in this esoteric account he gives of his persecutions, that he was "suspected," like Aponus, of entertaining opinions adverse to the superstition of the time. See the thirteenth chapter of *Secrets Revealed, or an Open Way to the Shut Palace of the King*, which now, in this age, may be interpreted, an open way to the knowledge of God.

This work was written by Eyrenæus Philalethes (Cosmopolita), and Dr. Mackay gravely informs us, as a precious item of actual history, that he kept some "philosophic powder in a little gold box," with "one *grain* (?) of which he could make five hundred ducats, or a thousand rix dollars"; that "he generally made his projection upon *Quicksilver*," — with many more absurdities.

Eyrenæus no doubt made his *projections* upon *Quicksilver;* that is, he sought to improve man through his conscience, as knowing that, "when that is safe, all is safe; but that lost, all is lost."

Everywhere in this secret philosophy we meet with the same doctrine, which may be expressed in the very brief sentences, Be just, be honest, be true, be faithful; Keep thy heart with all diligence, for out of it are the issues of life.

Dr. Mackay, in his sketch of Arnold de Villa Nova, a great name among the Alchemists, says: —

"In a very curious work by Monsieur Longeville Harcouet, entitled, *The History of Persons who have lived several Centuries and then grown young again,* there is a receipt said to have been given by Arnold de Villaneuve, by means of which any one might prolong his life for a few hundred years or so. In the first place, say Arnold and Monsieur Harcouet, 'the person intending so to prolong his life must rub himself well, two or three times a week, with the juice or marrow of Cassia (moëlle de la casse). [Formerly, gentle reader, *cassia* was medicinally used as a purgative, and here signifies that cleansing process of which all of the Alchemists write, a moral but not a physical cleansing. The receipt then proceeds:] Every night upon going to bed, he must put upon his HEART a plaster [this was indeed a funny way to make gold! a plaster] composed of a certain quantity [doubtless the exact size of "a piece of chalk"] of Oriental saffron, red rose-leaves, sandal-wood, aloes, and amber, liquefied in oil of roses, and the best white wax. In the morning he must take it off and enclose it carefully in a leaden box till the next night, when it must be again applied.'"

It never occurred to Dr. Mackay, that whoever would live happily, and prosperously, and healthily too, must go to bed with a pure heart, which also must be carefully preserved during the day.

This was the language by which men communicated with each other all over Europe, and encouraged each other to live honestly, when, in the public estimation, it was necessary rather to say a "certain" number of masses, and contribute largely to an ignorant, debauched, and wicked priesthood, armed with the civil power to crush all opposition to the tyranny by which they enslaved the whole population of Europe.

Has it no interest for this age to look back a few

hundred years, and see the shifts to which men were obliged to resort for the privilege of living with simple honesty? and is it surprising that this great privilege should be so highly exalted, and described as a stone of great price, — the Philosopher's Stone? What shall a man give in exchange for his soul? or what doth it profit a man, if he shall gain the whole world, and yet live in a state of self-condemnation?

The times are changed now, and it should be openly declared that the Alchemists were not the fools their foolish and silly *literal* readers have taken them for; but they were the wise men of their times, who couched their wisdom in "dark sayings," calculated purposely to mystify and deceive those who needed the "hangman's whip" to hold them in order, and no less to delude and elude the hangman too, who knew not how to discriminate between the true man and the false.

The times, I say, are wonderfully changed, and men can now declare their opinions openly and freely, if only it be done with decency and sincerity. Swedenborg, though he felt the convenience of writing mystically, said that God is a man; Fichte says man is a God, while Hegel says both are one. Comte publishes works of almost professed Atheism, and Feuerbach openly discusses the dogma that Theology is Anthropology. Some few read these books and take interest in them or throw them aside, according to their taste or genius, while some spectators look on and see in these various efforts only the struggles of speculative men laboring to solve the mysterious problem of man, the Sphynx of the universe. None of these efforts, their authors being left alone, have disturbed the order of events: the sun rises and sets as before; seed-time and harvest have their due returns; and it is generally acknowledged that the trouble about free opinions has arisen simply from the vain attempt violently to interfere with and suppress them. The opinion of the "sage of Monticello" is now almost universally received, that error is not dangerous so long as reason is left free to combat it.

The real interest of man must be regarded as a power ever at work to secure itself; and this interest must for ever be opposed to whatever is false and mischievous, and must perpetually be employed in discovering and establishing the true, since herein alone is the true interest of man to be found.

Bishop Sherlock said that Christianity was as old as the creation, and that the Gospel was a republication of the Law of Nature. Most likely it was a similar idea that led the Alchemists to claim that their Art was as old as the world; which can only mean that man from the earliest time must always have been interested in himself, and anxious to discover "what was that good for the sons of men, which they should do under the heaven all the days of their life." (Eccles. ii. 3.) "The Preacher" concluded that the whole duty of man is comprised in the injunction to fear God and obey the commandments; and this has been echoed in all parts of the world, and in all ages. What, then, is to be understood by the commandments of God? When the Preacher announced this law, the commandments in the New Testament had neither been written nor declared, and when the new dispensation was announced, it is conceded on all hands that some portion, at least, of the ceremonial Law of the Old Testament was abrogated. Christ has told us that the whole Law and the Prophets is comprised in the love of God and of our neighbor; — God, with all our might and strength and soul, and our neighbor as ourself. By placing these injunctions side by side, we may see that the fear of God must be consistent with the love of God, and if we are to love God with *all* our heart, our love of our neighbor must be included in it. It is but trifling, however, to be critical about words, when we should be considering *things.*

There has been suggested a distinction between a law and a command of God, which seems important. The Laws of Nature are by some regarded as the eternal decrees of God, and, though unwritten, are the only certain measure of the commands of God. The commands may be either verbal or written. We have them as they were written by men as they were moved by the Holy Spirit. The Laws always become known to us coupled with conditions; as, — to draw an example from physical nature, — if an organic substance be subjected to fire, it shall be destroyed. This is the law, and the form of a command to protect us from it would interdict us from such exposure.

These two formulas, one of a law and the other of a command, whether in regard to physical or moral nature, may be thought to embrace or extend, theoretically, to all things by which man may be affected. From the nature of the case, a command always presupposes a law, and may always be referred to it and tested by it. This is what I understand by testing all doctrines by the "possibility of nature." All commands must be supposed given for our benefit, and have in view either to secure to us some good, or to protect us from some evil, and in either case because of some law, which, as the eternal decree of God, must be, like the nature of God, unalterable. We may disobey a command, but we cannot violate a law. If we disobey a command really founded on a law, we necessarily suffer the penalty of the law; which is only saying that the course of nature never alters. If, now, we construe the fear or the love of God as having reference to the Law, we may clearly see, theoretically, the importance of the text, that all things work together for good to them *that love God;* that is, to those who love God's Law, and keep it in their hearts, that is, in their conscience, which perpetually " bears witness."

On this ground we may see the beauty of that exquisite little volume published or brought into notice by Luther, *Theologia Germania,* in which we read that obedience to God is the only virtue; disobedience, the only sin; — at least, this is what I understand by testing doctrine also by " the possibility of nature."

So far as man can know the *Law,* the command based upon it will always seem reasonable and divine, and will find its sanction in the knowledge of the Law; and if " to keep the commandments " means to observe the *Law*, there can be no question as to our interest in it, and just as little, with those who love God, of its imperative obligation; but in the latter case only will the obedience be free, the will being subject to reason; for the freedom of man does not lie in his will, which is blind, but in its subordination to reason and conscience.

But where the Law is not known,—the condition of nearly all mankind, and, as to some laws, of the whole of mankind,—every man must more or less act under constraint and be subject to a secondary power expressed verbally or in writing.

Now, when the commands are deemed to be first in order, and the test of nature instead of being tested by nature, and are urged as imperative independently of all reference to the Law, and when, too, all inquiries as to the latter are interdicted,— this implies a state of hopeless intellectual slavery, which the Law of Nature avenges in her own way by the evils of which we read in past ages where this absurd principle has prevailed.

Yet for those who do not or cannot satisfy themselves as to the Law, it seems but mere prudence for them to observe the commands, if, only, these can be known, it being a mere common-sense presumption that they must originally have been grounded upon experience and observation, especially when they have been the object of reverence for ages.

As most men, from the condition of the world, the claims of labor for sustenance, &c., are precluded from seeking a knowledge of many of the laws under the influence of which they nevertheless live, it seems altogether necessary that they should have the benefit of past experience, as expressed in the commands, and hence it appears as a wrong to them to withdraw their reverence from it, and thus loosen its hold over them, exposing them thereby to manifold dangers.

This I take to be the real and permanent ground for a Hermetic or Secret Philosophy, through which men who have leisure may prosecute their inquiries into nature, and communicate their discoveries and opinions to each other, holding them always subject to correction by the "higher Law," which is never to be denied.

Hermetic Philosophy does not differ from philosophy in general, both having in view the discovery of nature, except that the former has been confined to those inquiries which relate more especially to the moral conduct of man; but here, the results of this philosophy may not differ practically from those depending upon traditional commands, the only difference being in the nature of the *Sanction*. The Hermetic Philosopher obeys the command because he knows the Law,—and he requires no other authority,—just as he keeps out of the fire, as soon as he knows its nature; but those who are ignorant of the Law are moved by the authority of tradition, or they are influenced by hope or fear, or by some other passion.

It is manifest that he who knows the Law has, in that knowledge alone, an inexpressibly valuable treasure; for he obeys freely what is called reason, which is nothing else but a knowledge of the Law, and this again is the knowledge of God, all natural laws being the eternal decrees of God, known and acknowledged as such, from which it is impossible to seduce them. Now the Law of Conscience being the Law of God in the soul of man, obedience to it, when truly known, becomes of the first importance for all men, no matter under what circumstances they may be placed; for man can never be placed under conditions which release him from either its presence or its authority.

But the knowledge of Law in general must always be limited, and the Hermetic Philosopher must always consider himself as engaged in a never-ending pursuit, though a pursuit ever leading him cheerfully onward in proportion to the sincerity and earnestness of his efforts.

Every man who enters upon this pursuit, that is, who seeks knowledge by a direct study of nature, disowning the claims of mere tradition, must prepare, as Espagnet says, to make a long journey; for, indeed, he enters upon an endless task, in the prosecution of which, however, he will continually find pleasure and satisfaction, so long as his endeavors are guided exclusively by a conscientious regard for the Truth, that is, for true Wisdom, — the Lady so passionately loved by Bruno, who preferred being burned at the stake to denying his Love. He must never, for an instant, depart from this principle; for, if he does, he must infallibly lose his way, and may find his return next to impossible. Hence the perpetual cautions of the Alchemists, to wash and cleanse the matter of which the Stone is to be made, since whatever other light be followed, traditionary authority being neglected, will necessarily prove an *ignis fatuus*, which in the end will abandon those who depend upon it.

Here is the secret of all those lamentations over the vanities of this world, as riches, honors, and pleasures; not because these things are wrong in themselves, but because they are allowed the foremost place in the affections, to the suppression or exclusion of the divine Law of the Conscience.

It can hardly be said that there is a *doctrine* of Hermetic Philosophy; it is properly a *practice*, and it is the practice of truth, justice, goodness, or, in one time-honored word, virtue; the *End* being disclosed in the experience of the adept, but with the continued presence of self-approbation, provided this be under no circumstances compromised.

It was no doubt in view of this, that Sandivogius was led to express the opinion, that "many men of good consciences and affections secretly enjoy this gift of God"; for, it must be admitted, and it is worthy of all thankfulness, that every truly upright man must live, to the extent of his fidelity to the Law of God, under a sense of God's approbation; which may be as good a definition of the Philosopher's Stone as we need have. Merely learned men should know that they have no prescriptive or exclusive right to God's approval, but that this is the meed only of the honest man, whether he be clothed in silken robes or in the humblest apparel of the poor. This is the Elixir and the Water of Life, and the medicine so much talked of under the name of the Philosopher's

Stone, — at least, practically considered; though theoretically it may point to a special knowledge of 1, 2, 3, and 1, not to be expressed in words.

This being so, we may understand why all of the writers say that the profane cannot share it; for, in so far as a man departs from truth and rectitude, he departs from paradise.

It is a special distinction of this philosophy, that it does not waste its strength upon insoluble problems as to either the origin or the destiny of man; but, taking man as he is, it seizes upon the heart and conscience, and burying itself there, as it were, it lives altogether in the effort to purify and perfect this source of the issues of Life.

It need not be imagined that such a doctrine addresses itself to human pride, and power, and presupposes an independent ability in man to sustain and support himself. A very slight acquaintance with this philosophy will show the contrary, and will teach the student that all power is in God, which contains the power of man, just as the love of God contains the love of man. The power of man is defined by his knowledge of God, — his acceptance of it, and his submission to it. A right view of this will explain the difference between the power and the weakness of man, the former being measured by reason, and the latter by passion. Reason, in its nature, is above the phenomenal man, but yet not foreign to the whole man, and may be appropriated by a due submission to it, when, then, it raises man to itself, his proper home; which I understand as the true sense of 1 Cor. xv. 43. Passion, on the other hand, it has been well said, manifests the weakness of man; for through it man is under the dominion of agencies in nature, acting blindly and not according to light. Men under such influences are first the dupes of their own passions, and are then prepared to be the dupes of others.

It is a noble proposition in a work not yet published in English, though the author has been ignorantly abused in good modern Saxon for some two hundred years, that "we may be determined by reason alone to all of the *actions* to which we are determined by a passion." (Prop. 59, Part 4.) Some men under the influence of passion do the things that reason sanctions, and which therefore reason itself may do; but they are, by this author, only called *actions*, as distinguished from *passions*, when done by reason. But reason never sanctions any mere passion, as such; for men under the influence of passion, even when externally the conduct is conformable to reason and virtue, always act blindly, under the control of what the ancient Platonics called our "irascible" nature, as something which ought to be "amputated" from us. But the Alchemists would "separate" nothing from the "matter" proper to its *nature*. They would have everything turned (transmuted) into a "*true Salt*"; that is, converted to reason through the conscience, for these two "know and love each other." (John Pontanus.)

True power is always exercised in the spirit of Hamlet's advice to the players, — "gently, and with a certain temperance in the very torrent, tempest, and whirlwind of passion." The passionless man is not the man of reason, but he in whom the passions are guided by reason, that is, by reason and conscience; for, as in God these are one, so in man they should perpetually tend to union, the end and aim of all this doctrine. In the same sense in which the power of man is part of the power of God, and the love of man is part of the love of God, so is the conscience in man a part of the justice of God; and a right understanding of any one of these will explain all.

I am not sure but that I ought to explain more

particularly than I have yet done, that many of the Alchemists, in their works, while indicating the *subject* of their Art in their obscure way, speak of it sometimes as *one*, omitting the word *thing;* then, perhaps, as *two;* then as *three*, and as *four*, and finally as *five;* and yet affirm that there is no contradiction in this. They mean by *one*, the one universal or absolute existence, what Swedenborg and some other writers have called Substance. By *two* they mean the macrocosm and microcosm; or they mean the active and passive principles in nature; or they mean spirit and matter, or Soul and Body, &c. By *three* they add to the two principles a third as the *tie* of the two, which is really the *one*, which, with the two, makes their trinity of principles, 3 in 1. By *four* they mean the four so-called elements, earth, water, air, and fire, as if all things in nature were composed of these. By *five* they consider, in addition to the four, a fifth, or quintessence, as the unity of the whole.

With regard to the four, it should be observed, that it is not important to their theory that there should be just four elements, and no more, so that the modern discoveries of many so-called elements do not affect their theory; for they all saw that the so-called four elements were not independent of each other; that earth contains water, and water air, &c.; and in fact they expressly say that each contains all the others, in varying proportions. By saying that their subject is four, they only mean to direct attention to nature, though they study nature in or through man.

Some of the writers speak of the four elements as *natures* capable of passing one into another, from the observation of which some of them took the hint for what they call transmutation. One of them says:—

"Those that are ignorant of the causes of things may wonder with astonishment, when they consider that the world is nothing but a continual metamorphosis; they may marvel that the seeds of things perfectly digested should end in perfect whiteness. Let the philosopher imitate nature."

This circular operation of nature is now fully recognized by agricultural chemists.

Mr. Grove's recent announcement of his proposition would have been highly acceptable to the Alchemists, to wit, — as he states it in his *Correlation of Physical Forces* (3d ed., 1855, page 15), — "The position which I seek to establish in this Essay is, that the various affections of matter which constitute the main objects of experimental physics, viz. heat, light, electricity, magnetism, chemical affinity, and motion, are all correlative, or have a reciprocal dependence; that neither, taken abstractedly, can be said to be the essential cause of the others, but that either may produce, or be convertible into, any of the others: thus heat may mediately or immediately produce electricity; electricity may produce heat; and so of the rest, each merging itself as the force it produces becomes developed: and that the same must hold good of other forces, it being an irresistible inference from observed phenomena, that a force cannot originate otherwise than by devolution from some pre-existing force or forces."

On page 13 Mr. Grove says, that "The actual priority of cause to effect has been doubted, and their simultaneity argued with much ability."

This was undoubtedly the opinion of the Alchemists, and was applied by them to that experience which in the Sacred Scriptures is called the new birth, — by them symbolized under the figure of the transmutation of metals, which they all speak of as *one operation.* They illustrate it by the mingling of sugar with water, in which operation, if it be said that water changes the sugar, with the same reason it may be said that the sugar changes the water; and that there "is but one operation of both." A right conception of this will show how they considered the Love of God as one (thing), and that this Love is the same, whether regarded as the Love of God for man or the Love of man for God; the realization of which is the end of the "Work."

This notion may seem ridiculous, but those who study Hermetic Philosophy will find it to be a true exposition of the doctrine, whether the doctrine itself be true or not.

It may be desired that some account of the books of the Alchemists should be given beyond what is to be drawn from the extracts I have made from some few of their writings; but this cannot be done in a brief space, and I fear that my remarks have already been extended too far. If any one should desire to see an enumeration of their works, they may consult the third volume of Du Fresnoy's *Histoire de la Philosophie Hermetique*, where nearly a thousand authors are named; and we may readily suppose that a large number must necessarily have been omitted. Of these, it would be idle to imagine that the whole can have value, even supposing the Hermetic Philosophy a substantial reality. If, from the large number of authors upon the subject, a small number could be selected with judgment, and the remainder destroyed, there would be less difficulty in ascertaining the true ground of procedure, and the nature and extent of the results might be more easily estimated.

In the Chronological Table of some of the most distinguished Chemists (Alchemists or Hermetic Philosophers), Du Fresnoy enumerates ten before Christ. After Christ, and down to A. D. 1000, he enumerates twenty-one, after which period the number increases rapidly: in the eleventh century he names five; in the twelfth century, only three; but in the thirteenth century, eleven; in the fourteenth century, fifteen; in the fifteenth century, seventeen; in the sixteenth century, thirty; and in the seventeenth century, sixty-seven. But in this list a vast number of anonymous authors must have been omitted.

It is remarkable that Plato, in his *Seventh Letter*, notwithstanding he wrote a great deal himself, says, that "the truth with respect to "Nature" "lies in the smallest compass," and is of such a character, that "there is no fear that any one will ever forget it, who has once comprehended it by the soul"; — which may console some of us when we feel how impossible it is to read all the books in the world! Plato has taken care to point out the difference between the truth as it is in the soul, and the word, as it is written; as we may see in many places in his Dialogues, but especially towards the conclusion of *Phædrus*.

If all the books in the world were to be destroyed, the nature of man would reproduce them, or replace them with others of similar character; and as he who values the creature before the Creator inverts the order of things, so he who prizes human works before the spirit in which they have their birth commits the same error.

The Alchemists, or Hermetic Philosophers, appear to have been students of Plato. They quote Aristotle indeed frequently, but it is not certain always that they refer to known works of Alexander's teacher, for it is well understood that many alchemical works were written under assumed names, or were attributed to men who had attained celebrity in the world. A saying of Aristotle's in regard to one of his works — that it was published and not published, referring to its Hermetic or Esoteric character — might possibly have induced some of the symbol-writers of a later age to affix his name to their works. Be this as it may, my reason for supposing that the Alchemists were students of Plato is not so much derived from references directly to the writings of Plato, as to similitude of doctrine in some important points.

The Alchemists never name their *subject* directly; or, when they do so, they tell us that it is to deceive the profane, as when they compare it to *man;* for though man is the real subject of the Art, they pretend that they only speak of him as the subject by comparison or similitude; as may be seen by the passages cited from Flammel. They refer to the *subject* by calling it the *matter*, the *body*, the *two bodies* (Soul and Body), or they often use the mere pronoun *it*. They will say, for example, in their *receipts*, which may always be considered *deceits* (tubs): "Take the matter, *which you know* [when the general reader knows nothing of it], and purify it; you must see that it is perfectly clean, for nothing impure must enter into it," &c. A novice, by such language, is thrown off his guard, and has no idea that the *matter* is himself, and that the interpretation is, — If you wish to succeed in this Art, purify yourself; wash you; make you clean, &c.; or, if you wish to improve another, work on the same principle. This is Platonic doctrine, and nothing but plain good sense. It is explained very minutely in the Sophist, where erroneous opinions of all sorts are called "impediments" to true knowledge; and it is said they must be removed, and the person holding them must be "purified," and brought to "shame" with respect to them, before he is in a fit condition to receive true knowledge.

This bringing a man to "shame," as Plato calls it, is what the Alchemists call bringing about the *black state of the matter* (*dissolution, calcination,* &c.); and they tell us that it must necessarily precede the *white* state, before the latter can be genuine and bear the *test* of the coupel. This white state, they then say, contains the red state; for they work from within outwards, and deny with the greatest emphasis that goodness and truth can be put *upon* any one: it must be brought out of the subject, *à la Socratic obstetrics* (Theætetus); on the principle that "nothing can give what it has not."

It may be imagined, from the simplicity of the explanation, that there was nothing in Hermeticism to require or justify so much mystery and secrecy. But no one will hold to this opinion who understands that "the still, small voice" has actually more "pondus" than can be overcome by the whole world. It was held to be of such importance as to weigh down the entire claims of the external Church of the time. It may be said in some sense always to rise above the age in which a man lives, just as the ideal in all of the arts excels the practical, of which it is the measure. In this connection I would earnestly recommend the study of Plato's immortal *Seventh Letter* (4th vol. Bohn's edition).

It must be recollected that the Alchemists were Protestants, when Protestantism could not speak openly. Who cannot see — at least when it is pointed out — to what Eyrenæus refers when he says: —

"My heart murmureth things unheard of; my spirit beats within my breast for the good of all *Israel*. These things I send before into the world, like a preacher, that I may not be buried unprofitably in the world. Let my book, therefore, be the *forerunner* of *Elias*, which may prepare the kingly way of the Lord. I would to God that every ingenious man in the whole earth understood this science; . . . . . then would virtue, naked as it is, be held in great honor merely for its own amiable nature"; — almost as if the spirit of John the Baptist had warmed him into a prophecy of the full maturity of the Reformation; which is still incomplete, though it has been fermenting and working over three hundred years.

But I must bring these remarks to a close.

My purpose has been to show that, notwithstanding there were pretenders and impostors, and freely admitting that multitudes were deceived by the literal signification of the language of the Alchemists, the genuine adepts were in pursuit of neither wealth nor worldly honors, but were searchers after truth, in the highest sense of this word; and whether we call it truth, virtue, wisdom, religion, or the knowledge of God, one answer will be found to explain all of these expressions. This one answer, or one thing, was the Philosopher's Stone, and can be found in no other thing in the universe but the nature of man, made in the image of God.

Hence the importance of the maxim, KNOW THYSELF.

SINCE preparing the foregoing remarks, a friend has suggested that the *object* of the Alchemists is not explained with sufficient clearness. The query still remains, — What was the precise purpose of the Alchemists?

I do not well see how I can answer this any more fully than I have already done.

The reader will please observe that my first position is a negative one; viz. that the genuine Alchemists were not in pursuit of either riches or honors, in a worldly sense. To establish this point, I suppose nothing more is required than a bare perusal of the extracts I have given from the actual writings of the Alchemists. Those who desire more evidence, and persist in the ordinary opinion, must be left in their delusion, for delusion it certainly is.

This negative point may not of itself be of much importance; but it prepares the way for an inquiry as to the real object.

Of this I have given the opinion, that it was the perfection, or at least the improvement, of man; and I have indicated that, according to the theory of the writers, this perfection lies in a certain unity, I might say a living sense of the unity, of the human with the divine nature, the attainment of which I can liken to nothing so well as to that experience known in religion as the NEW BIRTH, however much this doctrine may be misunderstood and derided by zealots on the one side and the worldly-minded on the other.

I have endeavored to suggest that the desired perfection, or unity, is a state of the soul, *a condition of Being*, and not a mere condition of Knowing.

I regard this condition of Being as a development of the nature of man from within, — in some sense unattainable from without, except as external influences may administer occasions for its realization. I consider it the result of a process or practice, by which whatever is evil in our nature is cast out or suppressed, under the name of "superfluities," and the good thereby allowed opportunity for free activity according to its nature; but as this result is scarcely accessible to the unassisted natural man, and requires the concurrence of divine power, it is called *Donum Dei*, the gift of God.

Until experienced, the *conditions* of its existence require on the part of the philosophic neophyte something analogous to faith in religion; and because the *conditions* appear to be in contradiction to nature, or within themselves, one with respect to another, the resulting experience is said to be supernatural; but it only appears so when nature is conceived in a narrow sense, under definitions by which nature itself is divided and contemplated in parts, and not as a whole; but not so when we accept and realize the dogma, that nature contains nature.

If nature be defined the material universe, or

universe of matter, then it must be regarded as a blind, inert existence; but if the definition be extended so as to include its life, or power of Being and action, then that which under the former definition would be regarded as supernatural must be considered as included in nature; not that what is *actual* in Being can in any manner be affected by arbitrary definitions; but by means of these definitions the mind may be assisted to the formation of clear ideas about what at first we really have only imaginations or notions of, resting upon mere *names* and not *things*. Most men have, of course, notions of what they call *natural* and *supernatural;* but before these notions can be transmuted into ideas, they must be temporarily brought into question under a distinct and quite peculiar state of mind, which, itself, not being a result of the will directly, is for this reason alone often considered supernatural, though in the end it is recognized as within nature; or, perhaps it may preferably be said, not that the supernatural is brought down to nature, but that nature is elevated into the divine.

If the natural and supernatural be treated of by symbols, and called, the one *sulphur* and the other *mercury*, the mind of the student, forced to think of things instead of mere words, may be led finally to conceive the inseparable nature of the two in a certain third something, which, during the progress of the inquiry, may be called *Sol;* but as the three are seen to be indissolubly one, the terms may be used interchangeably until, "*after long contemplation of the subject, and living with it, a light is kindled on a sudden, as if from a leaping fire, and, being engendered in the soul, feeds itself upon itself.*" (Plato.)

Those who have never had this experience are apt to decry it as imaginary; but those who enter into it know that they have entered into a higher life, or feel enabled by it to look upon things from a higher point of view. (See the opening of the Second Book of Lucretius, finely used by Lord Bacon in the Essay on Truth.) To use what may seem a misapplication of language, it is a supernatural birth, *naturally entered upon;* it is the new birth of the Scriptures, brought about supernaturally *according to nature.*

In excuse for this language I would ask any one to weigh carefully the treatment of this subject by any eminent divine, and observe how language struggles in vain to escape the difficulties of it. As an example at hand, I will refer to the *Select Discourses* of the Rev. John Heylyn, D. D. (London, 1760), — the Discourse on Conversion, — an excellent work.

The text is from Zechariah i. 3: *Turn ye unto me, saith the Lord of Hosts, and I will turn unto you.*

In the treatment of this text, the writer labors under insuperable difficulties from the impossibility of avoiding the seeming contradiction, wherein it is required of man, as a condition of God's turning to him, that man shall turn to God; while yet this turning of man to God is not possible, but by the power of God in man.

We find in this Discourse the prayer, very appropriately introduced, — *Turn thou us, O good Lord, and so shall we be turned;* which presents directly the antagonism to the text.

The same antagonism is brought out by two other passages from Scripture: — *Him who cometh to me, I will not reject, I will in no wise cast out.* This supposes a natural power in man so to "come"; but then we read that *No man can come to me, except the Father, which hath sent me, draw him,* which affirms an impossibility in the natural man to move without supernatural help.

Let these two seemingly opposite or contradictory conditions be examined under any symbolic names the student pleases, the seeker keeping his *intent* upon things, and not words, and they may finally become reconciled in a certain third something, which shall be as the unity of the two, when all becomes clear.

As another example from Dr. Heylyn, consider the following passage: — " In strict reasoning, perhaps we ought not to ascribe locality to the Deity. *Human language cannot treat of God but with great improprieties.* Yet to say that we must seek God within ourselves, in our hearts, is in some respects a proper way of speaking, because it is a proper way of conceiving about God. God is in the Heavens, and above all Heavens: He is also in every tree, and plant, and stone, as verily as he is in the heart of man: He is in every other man's heart, as well as in ours. But seeing he is *within us*, we ought not to seek him *without us*. *He is a God near at hand, and not afar off.* Jer. xxiii. He is indeed both near and afar off by his Ubiquity or Omnipresence; but inasmuch as concerns us, inasmuch as he is *our* God, He is near us, *He is* IN *us*."

In this passage the word Heart is really a symbolic expression, and can only mean *that*, whatever it be, which may witness to us the presence of God in us. Our familiarity with this expression makes us feel, in the use of it, as if we knew all about it, though in truth we may know nothing about it. The Alchemists symbolize something similar by the expressions *philosophical mercury* and *philosophical gold*, the one being something in man, the other something in God, which are ultimately conceived as "one only thing."

By this symbolism the Alchemists escape, or endeavor to escape, the difficulty of treating the subject in ordinary language; for the meaning of the terms employed must be sought in the nature of things; or, as they warn us, must be tested by "the possibility of nature." They tell us, that whoever departs from nature is lost, and must commence his work anew. "Whoever is without the bounds of nature," says Espagnet, "is in error, or near one."

No direct language can grapple with the difficulties of this subject, and its use is calculated to throw a stumbling-block in the way of honest inquirers, while it furnishes a pretence to those who are disposed to cavil, and who think more of being subtle about words than of realizing the truth of things. But by symbolism these difficulties may to some extent be overcome, and this, too, without real injury to the student, who is perpetually cautioned by the Alchemists to accept only the truth, which he must test by a certain *infallible rule.*

It is true that here we encounter the very same difficulty in another form; for this *rule* is that very *truth* itself which the student is supposed to be seeking.

How, then, is the difficulty said to be overcome? I say to some extent; for, as by the literal language of symbolism no sense is attainable, or a very trivial one only, the student escapes the danger of being led to *fancy* that, by passing his eyes over a mere collocation of words, he has reached what Plato calls "the very wise thing itself"; and then, being driven back upon nature and himself, he may find what he seeks; or, rather, he is rewarded according to what he seeks;—*with the truth*, if that be his object, pursued with a "single eye"; but if his eye be "double," he finds nothing, for in this case he deserves nothing from the Art. At the worst, if the student understands the works literally, reading with a double eye, he misses indeed the wealth, the wisdom, which by supposition he is not seeking; but by experiments upon metals in pursuit of merchantable gold, instead of treasures not to be purchased, he unconsciously prepares the way for the useful science of chemistry, and so illustrates the beneficence of Providence in bringing good out of all things.

In reading a work written in symbols, the student is forced, I say, to consider things, and not words; and this allows his real desire (love, or purpose) to work itself out according to its essential nature. If this *essence* of the man, as Swedenborg calls it, is of the "superior" nature, "it produces that good from itself which it supposes it finds." By this process the student may be led into the right position for receiving a *certain experience*, which becomes as a light in the soul for the explanation of what seem contradictions to the "natural man." But they only appear to be contradictions because of the absence of the experience; somewhat as other experiences may be regarded as revelations and supernatural prior to their realization in life. Thus, the whole of life is supernatural to the helpless infant; not so much to the youth, in whom the powers of nature have begun to unfold themselves; while to the sage, "the common has become extraordinary, the extraordinary common," and God is recognized in all things; for to the sage all things are "full of God."

When the student, or more properly the "seeker,"

is in a right state for the reception of this experience, — for it has its fitting time and requires its suitable conditions, like all other things, — the Light comes to him, or rather rises within him; but as if from without, and may be said to be both natural and supernatural. The *Sulphur* and *Mercury* become one, or are seen to be the same, differing only in a certain relation; somewhat as the known and the unknown are but one, the unknown decreasing as the known increases, and *vice versa.*

The general reader may be reminded, by what is said of experience, of the very profound definition, to wit, that experience is that which one experiences when he experiences his experience. But a downright experience is not to be put out of countenance by a witticism, though from the monarch of modern literature.

"Internal illumination," says Menzel, "which, though the fruit of long preparation, yet remains an involuntary one, is a matter of fact, on which no false systems nor irrational claims should be founded: which should by no means be put to an ill use, but which yet can by no means be reasoned away"; — and what is more, it cannot even be ridiculed away. Locke tried his reason upon it, and Butler his wit; but the thing remains a universal fact, upon which, it is admitted, no false systems nor irrational claims should be founded; but this does not exclude inquiry about it, but rather invites it; for as a single fact it is the most extraordinary thing in the world.

Of course the use of the mere figurative word *Light* can teach nothing, and must be understood in regard to this subject as in respect to others, where we speak of the *light* of knowledge, the light of the understanding, and as it is used in the Psalms, *in thy Light shall we see Light*, which means, in thy truth shall we see truth; or, in other words, we know we have the truth when we realize it as in God,—which follows readily when we understand in what sense God is said to be Truth. Whoever sees the truth of a proposition, even of mathematics, as that a sphere is two thirds of its circumscribing cylinder, may form some notion of the Light in question, which teaches the relation of man to God, where the proposition takes precedence of all conceivable questions, and for this reason a sense of its solution must be realized as the purest and highest attainable Light, the sum and centre of all Light.

The importance attached to the personal state and purpose of the student is urged by these writers in the strongest manner. He is warned again and again to consider well what he seeks; for as everything has its proper cause, so things have also their proper effects, and the whole of nature is contained or expressed in some sense in these two dogmas; and yet, while each particular thing may be regarded as a single fact, from one point of view, it represents, from another point of view, an unvarying principle. Hence one of the writers says: —

"Thus, though I have somewhat metaphorically deciphered our true principles, yet I have done it so plainly that, with diligence, you may understand the meaning; and unless you know this, you will proceed blindfold in your work, not knowing the causes of things, so that every puff of sophisters will toss you, as a feather is tossed in the air with a blast of wind: for our books are full of obscurity: philosophers write horrid metaphors and riddles to those who are not upon a sure foundation, which like to a running stream will carry them down headlong into error and despair, from which they can never escape till they so far understand our writings as to discern the subject-matter of our secrets, which being known, the rest is not so hard. Proceed, therefore, not one step farther until you have learned this lesson, namely, to wed consanguinity with consanguinity [i. e. like nature with like nature], and consider well what it is you *desire* to produce, and according to that let be your intention. *Take the last thing in your intention for the first thing in your principles.* . . . . . . Attempt nothing out of its own nature [telling us, as usual, that grapes are not gathered from thistles, &c.]. . . . . . . If you apprehend this in its cause aright, and know how to apply this doctrine in your operation as you ought, you will find great benefit, and a door will hereby be opened to the discovery of greater mysteries."

The direction here given, to take the last *intention* for the first principle, is full of sound philosophy, though certainly a very simple thing in itself. It only means that a student should distinctly understand his ultimate purpose, there being a wide difference in the *state* of the individual who seeks what he seeks as an end, or as a means to an end. To seek knowledge for riches, is a very different thing from seeking riches (or independence) as an instrument of knowledge. In the study in question, the means and the end must coincide; that is, the Truth must be sought for itself only, and not as a means to another thing.

I have said that the instrument of preparation in

the work of Alchemy is the conscience, called by a thousand names, by means of which — become active as in the presence of God — the matter of the Stone (the Man) is first purified before it is possible for the Truth to be realized. By a metonymy the conscience itself is said to be purified, though in fact the conscience needs no purification, but only the man, to the end that the conscience may operate freely. The conscience under the name of a middle substance, in the language of the jargon, is said to partake of an *azurine* sulphur, that is, of a *heavenly* spirit, or in other words of the Spirit of God. It is this, as I conceive, which we are cautioned in a volume of universal authority not to grieve away.

Man first hears the voice of God in the conscience, the still, small voice, which, though often unheeded, is in Alchemy, as well as in the Scriptures, compared to a *fire:* — *Is not my word like as a fire, saith the Lord.* Jer. xxiii. 29. This prepares the way for what many of the writers speak of as a *Light*, the reference to which is so curiously wrapt up in figures and symbols, that I will cite an entire chapter on the subject, as a curious specimen of their mode of writing.

"CHAPTER III.*

"*Of the Regimen of Sol.*

"Now art thou drawing near to the close of thy work, and hast almost made an end of this business; all appears now like unto pure *gold;* and the *Virgin's Milk*, with which thou imbibest this matter is very citrine. [1 Cor. iii. 2. The conscience is very sound and healthy.]

"Now to God, the giver of all good, you must render immortal thanks, who hath brought this work on so far; and beg earnestly of him, that thy counsel mayest hereafter be so governed, that thou mayest not endeavor to hasten thy work; so as to lose all, now it is so near to perfection: consider that thou hast waited now about seven months, and it would be a mad thing to annihilate all in one hour: therefore be thou very wary; yea, so much the more by how much thou art nearer to perfection.

"But if thou do proceed warily in this Regimen, thou shalt meet with these notable things [experiences, symbolized, of an entrance into the higher Light or Life]: first, thou shalt observe a certain citrine sweat to stand upon thy Body; and after that citrine vapor, then shall thy Body below be

---

* From *Secrets Revealed*, by Eyrenæus.

tinctured of a *violet* color, with an obscure *purple* intermixed. [I must explain, that, when these works were written, physicians were in the habit of judging of the condition of their patients by the appearance of a certain water, and that a citrine color indicated a healthy condition, — here intended to signify the *moral* condition of the *matter* of the Stone: — the *violet* is the symbol of Love, and the *purple* of Immortality, — which are beginning to dawn upon the man in this stage of the work: — but to proceed.] After fourteen or fifteen days' expectation in this Regimen of Sol, thou shalt see the greatest part of thy matter humid [submissively yielding, — not by any force of will, but by a much more irresistible constraint, acting yet sweetly and not violently], and although it be very ponderous [self-willed], yet it will ascend in the Belly of the Wind. ["But when they arise or ascend," says Artephius, referring to the Soul and Body of the one man, "they are born or brought forth in the Air or Spirit, and in the same they are changed, and made Life with Life, so that they can never be separated, but are as water mixed with water. And therefore it is wisely said, that *the Stone is born of the Spirit*, because it is altogether spiritual." But to return to *Eyrenæus*.]

"At length, about the twenty-sixth day of this Regimen, it will begin to dry; and then it will liquefy and recongeal, and will grow liquid again an hundred times in a day [fluctuate between hopes and fears, assurances and doubts;—some of the writers say that, in this stage of the work, the *matter* will put on all the colors in the world, &c.], until at the last it will begin to turn into grains; and sometimes it will seem as if it were all *discontinuous* in grain, and then it will grow into *one mass* again: and thus it will put on innumerable forms in one day; and this will continue for the space of about two weeks.

"At the last, by the will of God, *a Light shall be sent upon thy matter, which thou canst not imagine.*

"Then expect a sudden end, which within three days thou shalt see; for thy matter shall *convert* itself into grains, as fine as the atoms of Sol, and the color will be the highest Red imaginable, which for its transcendent redness will show Blackish,— like unto the purest blood when it is congealed.

"*But thou must not believe that any such thing can be an exact parallel of our Elixir, for it is a* MARVELLOUS CREATURE, *not having its compare in the whole universe, nor anything exactly like it.*"

Descriptions similar to this may be found in all of the writings of the Alchemists in best repute among themselves. The author of the above wrote a Commentary upon Sir Geo. Ripley's *Compound of Alchemy*, expressly, as he tells us, that the reader might have the testimony of two combined. In this Commentary I find the following passages: —

"In the Beginning, therefore, of our Work, through the co-operation of heat [nature], both internal and external, and the moisture of the *Matter* concurring, our Body gives a Blackness like unto pitch, which for the most part happens at forty, or at most in fifty days.

"This color discovers plainly that the two natures are united. [By these *two* natures, the reader surely understands by this time, are meant what are called by innumerable names, Sol and Luna, gold and silver, Heaven and Earth, Phœbus and Daphne, superior and inferior, Soul and Body, &c., &c.] And if they are united, they will certainly operate one upon the other, and alter and change each other from thing to thing, and from state to state, until all come to one Nature and Substance Regenerate, which is a new Heavenly Body.

"But before there can be this renovation, the Old Man must necessarily be destroyed, [need I refer to

Eph. iv. 22-24, and Col. iii. 9, 10?] that is, thy first Body must rot and be corrupted, and lose its form, that it may have it repaid with a new form, which is a thousand times more noble. So then our Work is not a forced nor an apparent, but a natural and radical operation, in which our Natures are altered perfectly, in so much that the one and the other, having fully lost what they were before, yet without change of kind [without an absolute change of substance] they become a third thing, homogeneal to both the former.

"Thus they who sow in tears shall reap in joy; and he who goeth forth mourning, and carrying precious seed, shall return with an abundance of increase, with their hands filled with sheaves, and their mouths with the praises of the Lord. Thus the chosen or redeemed of the Lord shall return with songs, and everlasting joy shall be upon their heads, and sighing and sorrows shall fly away.

"Remember, then, this alchemic maxim, namely, that *a sad, cloudy morning begins a fair day and a cheerful noontide;* for our Work is properly to be compared to a day, in which the morning is dark and cloudy, so that the sun appears not. After that, the sky is overclouded, and the air cold with northerly winds, and much rain falls, which endures for its season; but after that the sun breaks out, and shines more and more, till all becomes dry; and then at noonday not a cloud appears, but all is clear from one end of the heaven to the other."

Here the author introduces cautions against haste and over-anxiety, advising patience, and proceeds: —

"Then shalt thou have leisure to contemplate these wonders of the Most High, and if they do not ravish and astonish thee in beholding them, *it is because God hath not intended this science to thee in Mercy, but in Judgment.* . . . . . Remember, then, when thou shalt see the renewing of these Natures, that with humble heart and bended knees thou praise and extol and magnify that gracious God, who hath been nigh unto thee, and heard thee, and directed thine operations, and enlightened thy judgment; for certainly flesh and blood never taught thee this, but it was the free gift of that God who giveth to whom he pleaseth. . . . . . This is the highest perfection to which any sublunary Body can be brought, by which we know that God is One, for God is perfection: — to which, whenever any creature arrives in its kind [according to its nature], it rejoiceth in Unity, in which there is no division nor alterity, but peace and rest without contention. . . . . .

"This is the last and noblest conjunction, in which all the mysteries of this microcosm have their consummation. This is by the wise called their Tetraptive conjunction, wherein the Quadrangle is reduced to a Circle, in the which there is neither beginning nor end. He that hath arrived here, may sit down at banquet with the Sun and Moon. This is the so highly commended *Stone* of the wise, which is without all fear of corruption. . . . . .

"*And this work is done without any laying on of hands, and very quickly, when the matters are prepared and made fit for it.* This work is therefore called a Divine Work."

In the Commentary upon the Fifth Gate of Ripley, the author, taking up the work in its more advanced state, says:—

"Thy Earth [meaning *Thyself*, addressing the Seeker] then being renewed, behold how it is decked with an admirable *green* color, which is then named the Philosopher's Vineyard. This *greenness*, after the perfect *whiteness*, is to thee a token that thy *matter* [thyself again] hath re-attained, through the will and power of the Almighty, a new Vegetative Life: observe then how this Philosophical Vine [thyself still] doth seem to flower, and to bring forth tender green clusters; know then that thou art now preparing for a rich vintage. [Col. i. 10.]

"Thy Stone [thyself] hath already passed through many hazards, and yet the danger is not quite over, although it be not great; for thy former experience may now guide thee, if rash joy do not make thee mad.

"Consider now that thou art in process to a new Work; and though in perfect *whiteness* thy Stone was incombustible, yet in continuing it on the Fire without moving, it is now become tender again: therefore, though it be not in so great a danger of Fire now as heretofore, yet immoderacy may and will certainly spoil all, and undo thy hopes: govern [thyself understood] with prudence, therefore, while these colors shall come and go, and be not either over-hasty, nor despondent, but wait the end with patience.

"For in a short time thou shalt find that this *green* will be overcome with Azure, and that by the pale wan color, which will at length come to a Citrine; which Citrine shall endure for the space of forty-six days.

"Then shall *the Heavenly Fire descend, and illuminate the Earth* [thyself] *with inconceivable glory;* the Crown of thy Labors shall be brought unto thee, when our *Sol* shall sit in the South, shining with redness incomparable.

"This is our true Light, our Earth glorified: rejoice now, for our King hath passed from death to Life, and possesseth the keys of both death and hell, and over him nothing now hath power. [Rev. i. 18.]

"As then it is with those who are redeemed, their Old Man is crucified, wherein is sorrow, anguish, grief, heartbreaking, and many tears; after which the New Man is restored, wherein is joy, shouting, clapping of hands, singing, and the like; for the ransomed of the Lord shall return with songs, and everlasting joy shall be on their heads: even so is it after a sort [the author means, precisely after this sort] in our operations; for first of all our Old Body dieth and rots, and is, as it were, corrupted, engendering most venomous exhalations, which is, as it were, the Purgatory of this Old Body, in which its corruption is overcome by a long and gentle decoction. And when it is once purged, and made clean and pure, then are the elements joined, and make one perfect, perpetual, indissoluble Unity; so that from henceforth there is nothing but concord and amity to be found in all our habitations.

"This is a noble step, from Hell to Heaven; from the bottom of the grave to the top of Power and Glory; from obscurity in Blackness, to resplendent whiteness; from the height of Venenosity, to the height of Medicine. O Nature! how dost thou alter things into things, casting down the high and mighty, and again exalting them from lowliness and humility! O Death! how art thou vanquished when thy prisoners are taken from thee, and carried to a state and place of immortality! This is the Lord's doing, and it is marvellous in our eyes." [Ps. cxviii. 23.]

The author then proceeds to illustrate the necessity of alternate action upon natural Bodies, before they can be prepared for a change of nature: they must be exposed to "heat" and "cold," must be "dried" and "watered" (prospered and saddened), in order to be made pliable and yielding, &c., &c., all of which must be done with one Fire, which he immediately calls the "*Spirit* proper to it," and then tells us that the wise men have called it their *Venus*, or *Goddess of Love*, and says:—

"Proceed, therefore, not as a fool, but as a wise man; make the water of thy Compound [thine own spirit] to arise and circulate, so long and often that the Soul, that is to say, the most subtle virtue of the Body, arise with it, circulating with the Spirit in manner of a Fiery Form, by which both the Spirit and Body are enforced to change their color and complexion: for it is this Soul of the *dissolved* Bodies, which is the subject of wonders; it is the Life, and therefore quickens the dead; it is the Vegetative Soul, and therefore it makes the dead and sealed Bodies, which in their own nature are barren, to fructify and bring forth. . . . . . If thou hast attended well to what hath been told thee in these five Gates, thou art secure; make sure of thy true Matter, which is no small thing to know, and though we have named it, yet we have done it so cunningly, that, if thou wilt be heedless, thou mayest sooner stumble at our books than at any thou ever didst read in thy life. Meddle with nothing out of kind [out of species or nature], whether Salts [generally called corrosives] or Sulphur, or whatever is of like imposition; and whatever is alien from the perfect metals [foreign to our nature] *is reprobate in our mastery*. Be not deceived either with receipts or Discourse, for we verily do not intend to deceive thee; but if you will be deceived, be deceived."

These writers have a favorite saying that *receipts are deceits*, and yet their books are filled with them;

but their receipts deceive no one who proceeds so far in the knowledge of their Art as to understand that it is not a work of the hands, but one of thought and meditation, with which the life must be kept in unison; for it is the destruction of the whole work not to have the thought and deed keep company, insuring in the end a perfect union of the intellect and will; for Sol and Luna must be indissolubly joined, and when this is done by nature, no Art can separate them.

If the few immediately preceding pages of *extracts* from the writings of the Alchemists are not sufficient of themselves to satisfy any one as to the general character of the object of the Art, and that it was religious, I know not what evidence would suffice for the purpose. There is but one subject in the whole range of human interests that can furnish an interpretation of these citations, and it is that which is known under the name of the *new birth* in religion. I admit that the experience itself may have many forms, the genuine element or substance of it breaking through a crust of human mixtures of innumerable components, as passions, errors, mistakes, ignorance, and sin, not forgetting also that it appears at various periods of life, sometimes as early as at six or eight years of age, and then again not unfrequently even at sixty and upwards.

It is stated, however, as a part of the history of the Art, that one adept found the Stone at twenty-three years of age, and this was thought a very early period of life for such a discovery; by which I am led to suppose that much of what is called a religious experience, or conversion, would not be considered as falling within the strict boundaries of the Art, or would not be regarded as a sure indication of being an adept.

I suppose a genuine religious experience is very rare, and that much of what commonly passes under this name indicates more of mere emotion than of true insight, and partakes more of human variability than the Art allows. The artists tell us to make the Stone once, and never make it again; meaning that, once truly made and there is no after change. We may even suppose them to mean that there is no falling from (a true) grace, and of course in that case there can be no repetition of it.

Some religious writers do not hesitate to say, that, if any one gives signs of having fallen from grace, it is a sure evidence that he never truly possessed it. I am not qualified to discuss this question, and yet I think its solution may have some bearing upon Alchemy. It may refer to what I call *the End* of the Art, of which I am religiously indisposed to speak, for many reasons, chiefly because no consideration in the world would induce me to hazard a mistake in regard to it; for whatever others may think of it, I suppose it to relate to the *one thing needful;* and as I would not willingly err on this point myself, so neither would I mislead any one in regard to it. I prefer to encounter the charge of presumption in recommending this abstinence for the imitation of others. He who undertakes the office of a teacher should at least be very sure of his own footing, especially in matters of religion, and I am sure that this is the subject of Alchemy.

I am in the belief that all of the genuine Alchemists were of the opinion that true religion cannot be taught, in the ordinary meaning of this word. It may be preached about, talked about, and written about; but there always remains something in the depths of a religious soul which cannot be expressed in human language. Hence the line,

"Expressive silence muse his praise,"

is the best utterance of a true religious feeling.

The subject of religion may be talked about, written about, and preached about; but the final step, the entrance into "light," is not taken by any force of mere human will, nor is it the reward of a mere search after knowledge, unless this search be after truth, as such, under an impulse which is not the fruit of any merely human will, but must itself partake of a religious character, its true nature only becoming known after it has consummated its own proper results. This I regard as one of the chief reasons for symbolic writing, as I have already said.

The Alchemists, as I have said, were earnestly employed about the NEW BIRTH, and though they called it *Donum Dei*, they inquired into it as a work of nature within nature; for with them it was a maxim that nature dissolves nature, nature joins nature, nature loves nature, nature amends nature, nature perfects and is perfected by nature. Therefore I have said that Alchemy was religious philosophy, or was so intended by the Alchemists, right or wrong, and that they were not in pursuit of gold.

Let them be condemned, if the reader pleases; but for what they were, and not for what they were not.

In religion, as popularly understood, conversion is said to commence with repentance, without which, we are told, it is impossible to reach a realizing sense of acceptance with God.

In Alchemy this repentance was called a "philosophical contrition"; which did not necessarily presuppose deliberate sin, but only such errors and mistakes as an unenlightened and unguided will must fall into in its first communion with the world. In this early stage the will regards chiefly the *individual self*, and its acts and doings tend to bring this self into conflict with the *not-self*, which is indeed only the other and really more noble part of the self, and the end is to turn the will to the *not-self* and adjust it to the whole, its *entire self*. Leibnitz says: "The human soul is infinitely richer than it is itself aware of: its being is so broad and deep, that it can never wholly develop and comprehend itself in the consciousness. Man is a mystery to himself, a riddle which will never be solved in the consciousness; for, should he ever attain to the internal intuition of his whole being, he would be swallowed up and consumed in himself."

The first steps of man towards the discovery of his *Whole Being*, the Alchemists called a philosophical contrition. They also called it the black state of the matter. This was said to be the first color, giving a sure sign of a true or right operation, without which the work could by no possibility succeed. In this black state was carried on the work of "dissolution," "calcination," "separation," &c., the separation being of that which the writers call the superfluous phlegm and fæces from the matter, which was then supposed to pass into the white state, — that of purification. In this white state the red was said to be contained, as the white was said to be contained in the black, the whole work being regarded as one continuous operation. The red state being wrought out advanced the matter to the perfect state, that of *Fixation*, as it was called; by which the soul was supposed to have entered into its true rest in God, where alone it can rest.

The so-called State of Fixation was not understood as one of unyielding reliance upon one's self, but as a condition in which the man was supposed *fixed* in an intelligent obedience to God, — fixed, because enabled to exclaim, If God be for us, who can be against us? But God is for those who know and obey his eternal will.

They compared man in this state to *wax* on a movable plane, maintaining its identity, not running like water, yet accommodating itself to the varying inclinations of the plane.

There appears to be something in the examination of this subject which opens up, at first, a seeming contradiction between the intellect and the senses, or between science and opinion, though in the end everything becomes reconciled in unity. We may perceive some shadow of it, in the evidence of the uninstructed senses that the heavenly bodies revolve around the earth, science ultimately showing that this movement of the heavenly bodies is only apparent, — a result of the revolution of the earth on its axis.

The most extraordinary results in mathematics have been obtained by a notion which the senses can in no wise conceive or comprehend, as in the differential calculus. Let the reader conceive a point in a circle, which, by definition, has no dimensions. To the senses there can be but one tangent to the circle at the point, but by assuming a right side and a left side to the point, or a motion of the point, which has no substantial dimensions, — a thing impossible to the imagination, — and then supposing two tangents through these imaginary sides of the point, an indefinitely small space is assumed to exist between the point and the two tangents; and this *may pass* for a fluxion, in the use of which — wholly inconceivable to the senses —

the most astonishing results have been obtained in mathematics; and no one can assign a limit to discoveries of this nature, in which the intellect, or a certain intuitive conception (not perception) overmasters the senses and carries them into willing captivity.

No one can define and distinguish eternity from time, so as to avoid the notion that eternity is a very long time. We call it infinite, and fancy that by this word we have removed the difficulty, but it is universally conceived as a double infinite, an infinite past and an infinite future; when, in fact, these expressions are wholly improper, both the past and the future being to the imagination indefinite, but not infinite; while the present, which is like the point in the circle, without dimensions to the senses, is said by some to be the true infinite, or the true eternal, for we *are* never *in* the past and never *in* the future, but always in the present, which may be called the *substance* of *time*, time itself, the past and future, being two "superficial components" of the eternal. If we call the present *Sol*, and the past and future *Sulphur* and *Mercury*, and study *the nature of the thing*, free from the bias of early education and habit, and free also from the delusion that words can teach things, when it is things only that can define words, we may discover how the present is the essential, while the past and future are superficial, and yet all three are one; for while in the present, we are in the future *with respect to the past*, and in the past *with respect to the future*.

Hobbes could not *perceive* this, and as he could not or did not *conceive* it, he ridiculed the notion of an eternal *Now*, — as he denied everything that refused to come under the dominion of the senses. But the history of science everywhere illustrates the proper supremacy of the intellect over the senses, and when attained in due course of nature itself, the senses become perfectly obedient, as we see emphatically in the history of astronomy.

It is entirely useless for opinion to enter into conflict with science, or sense with intellect; for the intellect cannot be convinced through or by the senses; neither indeed can the senses be convinced except through the intellect, and as most men live in the senses and not in the intellect, so most of the conscientious disputations in the world are confined to those who live wholly or chiefly in the senses; that is, upon opinions and not knowledge, in which both parties may be in error, while neither the one nor the other is able to distinguish where the error lies. But in true knowledge there is no ground for dissension and conflict, the very existence of which is proof that one or both of the parties has no proper conception of the point in debate.

From this comes the saying, that clever men soon discover each other and recognize each other by signs infinitely more sure and unfailing than any artificial or conventional signs in masonry or any other secret association.

I have thus endeavored to show that Alchemy — the name of Hermetic Philosophy in the Middle Ages — was religious philosophy, or philosophic religion; for here as elsewhere the Sulphur and Mercury (the Sun and Moon) pass into one.

It was an effort, in what has been called a benighted period, to realize religion apart from its forms and ceremonies, as properly innate in man, whose nature was supposed to contain it. In the language of Hollandus, " It contains all that we seek; and it needs only that, first, we separate what is superfluous from it, and then, that we turn its inside outwards: then it will be good gold."

But as this may seem to present an inviting

facility, as if it was an easy matter for man to be saved, — which the philosophers indeed tell us is really the case, but they add, that it is only so to the wise man, for to the wise man only is the yoke of Christ easy, — I will add two or three passages from a work entitled *De Manna Benedicto*, which may serve to show how earnest these writers were in their warnings against indulging in self-security and ungrounded hopes. The reader may remember the cautions of Espagnet and others already cited.

"Whosoever thou art that readest this Tract, let me advise thee rather to fix thy mind and soul on God, in keeping his commandments, than upon the love of this Art [the love, the author means, of the supposed external advantages of the Art], for although it be the only, nay, all the wisdom of the world, yet doth it come short of the divine wisdom of the Soul, which is the Love of God in keeping his commandments...... Hast thou been covetous, profane? be meek and holy, and serve in all humility thy most glorious Creator: *if thou dost not resolve to do this, thou dost but wash an Ethiopian white, and shalt waste an earthly estate, hoping to attain this science.*

"There is no human art or wit which can snatch it from the Almighty's hand; nor was it ever, and

I am persuaded it never shall be, given but to such as shall be of upright hearts."

As a further caution against precipitate haste in forming conclusions as to this philosophy, I will add the following passage from the commentary of Eyrenæus upon Ripley: —

"We have plainly and faithfully done our duty, and by a line, as it were, have separated the false from the true; yet we know, that in the world our writings shall prove as a curious edged knife: to some they shall carve out dainties, but to others they shall serve only to cut their fingers: yet we are not to be blamed; for *we do seriously admonish all who shall attempt this work, that they undertake the highest piece of philosophy in nature;* and though we write in English, yet our matter will be as hard as *Greek* to some, who will think nevertheless that they understand us well, when they misconstrue our meaning most perversely; for is it imaginable that they who are fools in nature, should be wise in our books, which are testimonies unto nature? ..... For all this work of the Artist is only to help nature; we can do no more; yea, we have professed and will continue to profess that we do but administer unto nature herein. For all the works of God are entire; we can but behold them and admire them" (and work with them), "and therefore we seek our *principles* where nature is, and amend nature in its own nature. Whereas those who work upon other matters do most shamefully betray their ignorance. They do not consider the possibility of nature, but work after their fancy."

This writer, Eyrenæus, compares a seeker to one who enters a castle, anxious to view its curiosities, which, however, cannot be seen but by means of a *guide*, who accordingly offers his services. This guide has a peculiar character, and the seeker is thus advised in regard to him: —

"You must know how to please him, that he may be the more willing to go along with you in the right way, and not leave you, as he hath done some, nor mislead you, as he hath done others, who, when they have attempted this work with fair success in the knowledge of matters requisite, have notwithstanding fatally erred, — not knowing how to please their *guide*, who hath a humor of his own not to be equalled in the world; *and if you make him either sullen or choleric, you may as well give over the enterprise.*

"First of all, then, know that for his part he is

a very stupid fool; there is none more simple among all his brethren; yet he is most faithful to his Lord, and doth all things for him most prudently, ordering all things in the family very discreetly;—which I may rather ascribe to a natural instinct, than to any quickness of parts. He is very faithful; for which cause he will never either ask or answer any question, but goes on his way silently: nor will he ever go before you, but follow. You must be very wary how you lead him, for if he can find an opportunity he will give you the slip, and leave you to a world of misfortune.

"By his countenance you shall know whether he be pleased or displeased; therefore lay bonds on him; that is, shut him close where he may not get forth: then go before with *heat*, and be ever watchful of his countenance as he follows; his anger you shall know by redness in his countenance; and his sullenness by his lumpish behavior; when in good humor he is indifferent active and merry: and so you shall pass on forward, or turn, or go back, as you see his countenance and temper inclined."

Need the reader be told who this personage is, and that every man hath him at command unless he offends him and drives him away, or by neglect reduces him to silence? He is the soothing "plaster" to be applied to the heart at night, and to be carefully preserved during the day; the use of which Dr. Mackay, LL. D., could not understand. He was the guide of Socrates, known in history as the *Dæmon of Socrates;* and the grand difference between Socrates and other men lies principally in the simple fact, that the teacher of Plato never disobeyed his guide.

Socrates, in his Defence before the Athenians, is made by Plato to speak of himself as being "*moved by a certain divine and spiritual influence,*" which he says began with him "*from childhood, being a kind of voice which even in the most trifling affairs*" opposed him, "*when about to do anything wrong,*" but never urged him on when in the right; that is, like the guide spoken of by Eyrenæus, never went before him, but kept him company, and put on a certain "redness of countenance" whenever danger was near.

Whole volumes and numberless essays have been written to explain the simple allusions in Plato and Xenophon to the Dæmon of Socrates; but nothing more is necessary for this purpose, than a reference to "*the possibility of nature,*" with a reasonable supposition that the conscience is more clear and distinct in its monitions to some men than to others, being perhaps less overlaid and obstructed in its action.

As this volume is purposely made up of extracts from the writings of the Alchemists, — to let them speak for themselves, — and has nothing of my own in it but suggestions with a view to the interpretation of those writings, I will cite another example of a reference to the conscience as *the guide* to what I call, for convenience, *the End.* I take it from *Lumen de Lumine,* or *a New Magical Light.* (1651.)

"There is a *Mountain* [Mons Magorum Invisibilis], situated in the midst of the Earth or Centre of the World [this centre is said to be everywhere], which is both small and great. It is soft; also above measure hard and stony. It is far off, and yet near at hand; but by the providence of God invisible. In it are hidden most ample treasures, which the world is not able to value." Here follows a picture of the difficulty of reaching this mount, with a statement, that it is to be found "by those that are worthy; but, notwithstanding, by every man's self-labor and endeavors." (Phil. ii. 12.) And the author proceeds: —

"To this mountain you shall go in a certain

night, when it comes, most long and most dark [the night of trial, doubt, trouble, — the dark wood of Dante]; and see that you prepare yourselves by prayer. Insist upon [pursue only] the way that leads to the Mountain, but ask not of any [mere] man where the way lies; follow only your *Guide*, who will offer himself to you, and will meet you in the way, but you shall not know him. [Very few, certainly, recognize the conscience as the oracle of God, — the guide to his presence.] This Guide will bring you to the Mountain at midnight, when all things are silent and dark [at the point of greatest depression in a worldly sense]. It is necessary that you arm yourself with a resolute, heroic courage, lest you fear those things that will happen [trials of the conscience] and so fall back. You need no sword [except that of the Spirit], nor any other bodily weapons; only call upon God sincerely and heartily. [Invoke the aid of the Greatest and Best.] . . . . . Be resolute, and take heed that you return not, for your Guide, who brought you hither, will not suffer any evil to befall you. [" No man, having put his hand to the plough, and looking back, is fit for the kingdom of God." Luke ix. 62.]

" As for the Treasure, it is not yet discovered, but it is very near."

Various trials are described, as violent winds, an earthquake, and a fire, "consuming the earthly rubbish," and then "after all these things, and near the daybreak, there shall be a great calm, and you shall see the day-star árise, the dawning will appear, and you shall perceive a great Treasure. [The *calm* is that of the soul surrendering itself to God.] The principal thing in it, and the most perfect, is a certain exalted *Tincture*, with which the world, if it served God, and were worthy of such gifts, might be tinged, and turned into most pure gold" (perfect goodness).

The Tincture we are directed to use as the "Guide shall teach," and it shall make the old young, &c., and pearls shall be discovered "of such excellency as cannot be imagined."

"But do not arrogate anything to yourselves because of your present power [1 Cor. iv. 6], but be contented with that which your *guide* [a pure conscience] shall communicate to you. Praise God perpetually for this his gift, and have a special care that you use it not for worldly pride, but employ it in such works as are contrary to the world. Use it rightly, and enjoy it so as if you had it not. [To use anything *rightly* is simply to use it conscientiously; — and no gift of God is a personal possession, but a trust, which is substantially lost the moment it is prized as an exclusive right. This is according to St. Paul.] Live a temperate life, and beware of all sin, otherwise your guide will forsake you, and you shall be deprived of this happiness. For know this of a truth, whosoever abuseth this Tincture, and lives not exemplary, purely, and devoutly before men, he shall lose this *benefit*, and scarce any hope will there be left ever to recover it afterwards."

There is no particular mystery in this concluding remark, since a conscience void of offence can be maintained only by avoiding offence. Many will think the simplicity of these directions is not worthy so much mystery and secrecy as these writers throw over it; but the attempt to put into practice what they teach may turn out to be the most difficult thing in the world. Beautiful things are as difficult as rare, says Plato. *Let him who standeth take heed lest he fall*, says a greater authority.

It must be observed that the guide is not the spectacle, but the way to it, as I understand these writers. The spectacle itself is said to be something altogether *unique*, with which nothing can be compared, and though at last " involuntary, it comes unsought to none": hence philosophy echoes the teaching in Matthew vii. 7, "Ask, and it shall be given you; seek, and ye shall find; knock, and it shall be opened unto you." But you *must* seek.

I commenced these Remarks with citations to show that man was the subject of Alchemy. I will here add another passage to this point, taken from Eyrenæus.

"Our STONE is the representative of the great world, and hath the virtues of that great fabric, comprised or collected in this little system. In it there is a virtue magnetical, attractive of its like in the whole world. It is the Celestial Virtue, expounded universally in the whole creation, but epitomized in this small map or abridgment.

"This Virtue or Power is in itself barren, sluggish, and inactive, and for this reason it remaineth without fruit; but being loosed by Art, it doth through the co-operation of Nature [often called *Fire* or *Heat*] produce that *Arcanum* which hath not its like in the whole world. . . . . . The reward which this Mastery will bring to the Artist, is indeed inestimable; for having it, he needs want no worldly blessing. For wealth he need take no care, and from all frailties of body he hath a most sure antidote.

"Pray then to God, that he would be propitious unto your studies and labors, in giving thee the true knowledge of this secret *mystery*. It is the gift of God. I have helped thee what I can, but VENTURE NOT TO PRACTISE BARELY UPON MY WORDS; for know that what I have only hinted, is far more than what I have explained; and what I have declared to thy first apprehension most openly, hath yet its lurking serpent under the green grass; I mean, some hidden thing which thou oughtest to understand, but which thou, being sure at first blush, wilt neglect, and then it will bite thee by the heel when thou approachest to practice, and make thee begin again, and, it may be, at last throw away all, as one desperate; for know that *this Art is very Cabalistical*, and we do study expressions such as we know will suit with almost any man's fancy, in one place or another; but be sure to take this maxim from one who knows best the sense of what he hath written: Where we speak most plainly, there be most circumspect; for we do not go about to betray the secrets of nature; especially then in those places which seem to give receipts as plain as you would desire, suspect either a metaphor, or else be sure that something or other is suppressed, which thou wilt hardly without inspiration ever find of thyself, and which in trial will make all thy confident knowledge vanish; yet to a Son of Art, we have written that which never heretofore was by any so clearly revealed."

Eyrenæus concludes his book upon Ripley, after a minute though cabalistical account of the *operations*, in these words: —

"The cause of all these strange alterations in one glass, on one subject, with one decoction, without any laying on of hands, lies in the *Internal Disposition of the Compound*, which at the first is gross and earthy [St. Paul's natural man, gentle reader]: therefore in decoction it becomes very black, it being the nature of all moist gross things by the Fire to acquire such a color. And this is according to the teaching of all Philosophers; for, although thou seekest White and Red, yet thou must at first make Black, before thou canst make White profitably.

"O Happy Gate of Blackness, which art the passage to this so great a change! Study, therefore, whoever appliest thyself to this Art, only to know this secret; for know this and know all, and, contrariwise, be ignorant of this and be ignorant of all.

"But when once thy Matter is become truly Black, rejoice; for this death of the Body will be the quickening of the Spirit, and then both Soul and Body will unite into a perfect whiteness, which is our *Kingly Diadem.*"

The death of the Body, to which reference is here and elsewhere made in these writings, I assume, of course, is that to which St. Paul refers; as, in Romans vi. 6, where he calls it the death of the Body of Sin.

I find a remarkable allusion to the triple nature of Man in Plutarch's Miscellanies (on Morals), and two deaths referred to as necessary for the liberation of man to bring him into a right state. The passage is so peculiar, that I will take leave to copy it as a curiosity, observing that the *Miscellanies* are full of the opinions of ancient philosophers upon the nature of man, having now but little more than an historical value. In the English translation, published in 1694, Plutarch sometimes is made to use the word *mind*, and sometimes *understanding*, for what is now often called *spirit:* in some places he uses the word *Discourse* as the *Word*, especially in *Isis and Osiris*, apparently in the sense of John i. 1.

The passage to which I refer occurs in the tract entitled *Of the Face appearing in the Orb of the Moon;* to wit:—

"The common opinion, and that which most persons hold, is, that Man is a compound subject; and this they have reason to believe. But they are mistaken in thinking him to be compounded of two parts only; for they imagine that the Understanding is a part of the Soul; but the Understanding as far exceeds the Soul, as the Soul is better and more divine than the Body. Now this composition of the Soul with the Understanding makes Reason; but with the Body, Passion; of which *this* is the beginning or principle of pleasure and pain, and *that* of virtue and vice. Of these three parts, conjoined and compacted together, the Earth has given the Body, the Moon the Soul, and the Sun the Understanding to the generation of man. Now, of the deaths we die, the one makes two of three, and the other one of two. And the former indeed is in the region and jurisdiction of *Ceres*, which is the reason of our sacrificing to her...... As for the other death, it is in the Moon, or region of Proserpina. And as with the one the Terrestrial, so with the other the Celestial *Mercury* inhabits. *This* suddenly and with force and violence plucks the Soul from the Body; but *Proserpina* mildly and in a long time disjoins the Understanding from the Soul. And for this reason is she called the *Only Begotten*, or rather, *Begetting One alone;* for the better part of Man becomes alone, when it is separated by her. Now both the one and the other happens according to Nature thus: [Here follow two or three pages of mystical explanation, and we encounter this passage:] —

"The Soul being moulded and formed by the Understanding, and itself moulding and forming the Body, by embracing it on every side, receives from it an impression and Form, so that, although it be separated both from the Understanding and the Body, it nevertheless so retains still its figure and semblance for a long time that it may with good right be called its image. . . . . . The Understanding is that which is sovereign over all the rest, and cannot be made to suffer by any."

In Plutarch's *Banquet of the Seven Wise Men*, the following passage occurs: —

"Since Thales has asserted the Being of a Soul in all the principal and most noble parts of the Universe, it is no wonder that the most commendable acts are governed by an overruling power, for as the Body is the organ of the Soul, so the Soul is an instrument in the hand of God. [In the previous extract this is called the Understanding.] Now as the Body has many motions of its own, proceeding from itself, but the best and most from the Soul, so the Soul acts some things by its own power, but in most things it is subordinate to the will and power of God whose glorious instrument it is."

In the *Discourse concerning the Dæmon of Socrates*, Plutarch introduces a speaker as saying: —

"Every Soul hath some portion of Reason [here Reason is used for the Understanding, that is, the Spirit, or, in other words, the Spirit of God]; a man cannot be a man without it; but as much as she mixes with flesh and appetite is changed; and through pain or pleasure becomes irrational. Every Soul doth not mix herself alike, for some plunge themselves into the Body, and so in this life their whole frame is corrupted by appetite and passion; others are mixed as to some part, but the purer part still remains without the Body; 't is not drawn down into it, but it swims above, and touches the extremest part of the man's head. 'T is like a cord to hold up, as long as it proves obedient, and is not overcome by the appetites of the flesh. The part that is plunged into the Body is called the Soul, but the uncorrupted part is called the Mind [Spirit], and the vulgar think it is within them, just as they imagine the image reflected from a glass to be in the glass; but the more intelligent, who know it to be without, call it a Dæmon."

We may observe in these extracts from Plutarch, which must not be understood as expressing his own opinions, for they occur in dialogues, how the *notion* of the *Spirit* (understanding, reason, or whatever it may be called) floats, as it were, between heaven and earth, one speaker placing it in man, another referring to it as out of man, acting upon him as the Spirit of God. I only cite these passages to show that the idea of a triple nature in man is not uncommon in the world; but I do not refer to them as a key to the opinions of the Alchemists.

From the writings of the latter I have brought together many extracts, and if any one can read them and still think that the authors were in pursuit of gold, I must leave him in his opinion. If he had lived in the age when the works were written, he would most likely have been among those who read them literally, and, so understanding them, sought the secret in metals. This was the class of men who gave occasion for the present reputation of the peculiar thinkers they so entirely misunderstood.

The author of these Remarks need not be told that there were false Alchemists, both those that were simply mistaken and those who impudently imposed upon the public. He contends that, notwithstanding the just reputation of this class of self-seekers, the genuine Alchemists were students of Nature, perfectly honest in their purposes, aiming at the *Summum Bonum;* and it may be well for those who in this age refuse all credit to their pretensions not to deny at the same time that God has placed within the reach of every man a true good, however difficult its discovery may be, or rather, however slow and apparently unwilling men may be to believe that it can be found in a true life. No one denies, indeed, theoretically, the value of a true life. It is universally admitted to be indispensable to a happy life, but almost all men place something else as first in order, although, when examined, that something turns out to be only a means to some end, whereas in a true life both the means and the end unite and become one.

The key, therefore, to a true life is nothing else but a true life itself; and this is the root of all philosophy which aims at the elevation of man, and, in fine, it is the root of truth itself, or rather it is root, body, and branches.

In vain, therefore, do men go out of themselves for that which can only be found within; and as this is both the oldest and newest truth in the world, so is it the most simple and open, while yet it is the most hidden and secret thing in the world, — open and simple to those who accept it in its own spirit, but dark and obscure when sought after as something to be found abroad, and to be *explained* and *understood*, as the expression is.

Yet as often as I refer to what may seem the simplicity of the work, I feel obliged to repeat that this is but *the Way;* the *End* being, as I understand the matter, a further development, the reward of those who "persevere *to the end* in welldoing."

When the Alchemists speak of a long life, as one of the gifts of the Stone, they mean immortality; when they attribute to the Stone the virtues of a universal medicine, the cure of all diseases, they mean to deny a positive nature to evil, and thus deny its perpetuity; when they tell us that the Stone is the "cut-throat of covetousness and of all evil desires," they mean that all evil affections disappear in the light of truth, as darkness yields to the presence of light.

They cultivated simplicity of life as a positive good, and systematically avoided all excesses, — all extremes. They even warn those who seek the

Stone, to pursue their studies with an unanxious patience and moderation; at the same time, however, they tell the seeker that his search must on no account be intermitted. Here, as elsewhere, they guard against extremes, cautioning the student neither to let his "matter grow cold," nor "to burn his flowers with too much heat."

Thus, to the maxim, KNOW THYSELF, they added its younger brother, NOTHING TOO MUCH; for as man occupies a middle position in Nature between the air and the earth, so the recognition and possession of a certain indescribable *mean* in his own nature may protect him from all vicious extremes, and secure the best ground of hope even here of a "sound mind in a sound body."

By the transmutation of metals, the Alchemists meant the conversion of man from a lower to a higher order of existence; from what is commonly called a natural, to a spiritual life, though these much used and little understood expressions cannot precisely make known their true meaning. By "fires," "menstruums," and many such expressions, they intended to signify the powers of nature, which, though separated in "number," were regarded as working in one nature, and therefore in *unison*, the writers with one voice denying that there is any absolute disorder in the works of God, where all "discord is harmony not understood."

The curious reader may see much of this very subject artistically illustrated in the fourteenth and fifteenth chapters of Carlyle's translation of the Travels of Wilhelm Meister, where the *Son of Anac, St. Christopher*, personates Nature, *reducing all minor harmonies to itself, and compelling those who "play out of tune" to come again into the general concord;* for Goethe was a cunning Alchemist in his way, and knew better than any modern writer how to screen his deepest thoughts in symbolism, which even Jeffrey, with all his talent, could not see through, as his criticism upon Wilhelm Meister sufficiently shows.

In saying a word or two of the *Fires*, I beg the reader to credit me when I declare that I only wish to show a probability that the writers intended to refer to the powers of and in nature; and that by the *Three* Fires, sometimes called *Menstruums*, and again, at times, called *Dissolvents*, they referred to their so-called *three* principles, or trinity in unity, the chief being of an "inseparable oneness" (the expression of Eyrenæus) yet having two "components," each of which being in its kind a *Fire* or menstruum, composed likewise of other two compounds passing into the first in some inexplicable way, though possibly to an imaginative reader not altogether inconceivable.

The "components" I suppose to be symbolized by Sol and Luna, as the active and passive principles of nature, or cause and effect included in one self-existence, and these same principles, I suppose, are alluded to by Goethe in the fourteenth chapter of Meister's Travels, where, undoubtedly, the author describes symbolically his own studies into the depths of nature; in the prosecution of which he is led to an extraordinary spectacle, in which he sees "*male* and *female* forms [the "components"], of gigantic power, in violent postures," which, he says, "reminded one of that lordly fight between heroic youths and Amazons, wherein hate and enmity at last issue in mutually regretful alliance."

These two principles are the two "great luminaries" referred to by Espagnet, there being nothing in nature without them, though the words Sol and Luna are applied to a great multitude of *doubles* besides what are sometimes called *natura naturans* and *natura naturata;* as, nature and man, &c., &c.

Eyrenæus speaks of the same two principles, and refers to their harmony in one other thing, including them both, as follows: —

"The *Bodies*"—everywhere, by the way, these writers thus speak of one, two, or three *somethings*, without telling the reader what the somethings are—"The Bodies, when they are *dissolved*, do transmute the foresaid mercuries, by their own ferment, into their own nature; for the Fire of Nature assimilates all that nourishes it to its own likeness; and then our Mercury or Menstrue vanishes, that is, it is swallowed up in the Solary Nature, and all together make but one universal *Mercury*, by intimate union, and this *Mercury* is the material principle of the Stone; for before, our *Mercury* (as it was compounded of three *mercuries*) had in it two which were superficial, and the third essential to Sol and Luna only, not to the Stone: for Nature would produce these two out of it by artificial decoction: but when the perfect Bodies are dissolved, they are transmuted with the *Mercury* that dissolved them, and then there is no more repugnancy in it,—then is there no longer a distinction between *superficial* and *essential*, but all becomes *essential*.

"And this is that one matter of the Stone; that *one thing* which is the subject of all wonders.

"When thou art come to this, then shalt thou no more discern a distinction between the *Dissolver* and the *Dissolved;* for the water shall neither ascend nor descend, go out nor in alone, but the Fire of Nature shall accompany it, and the color of the *mature Sulphur*, which is inseparably joined, shall tincture thy water; so that thou shalt never see them severed one from the other, but shall discern them by the effect, and by *the eye of thy mind*, more than of thy body."

As my object is to point out the *subject* of Alchemy, and as I neither expect to make its treatment plain, to *the end of the work*, nor to defend it, I will here add one or two passages from Plotinus, to show by a similitude of idea that the subject of Alchemy was the same as that of the Neo-Platonist, to wit, Man, and his relation to God.

Plotinus has been almost universally set down as a dreamer, and it is not my province to dissent from this very convenient resort for those who have no taste for the subjects he dealt with. Possibly the truth may be that Plotinus was himself less of a dreamer than many who have read his works through their own imaginations, for here lies a principal difficulty on this subject. If any one reads Plotinus, or Plato, or any other writer upon the topics they discussed, and forgets that the sources of truth are equally open to us all, he can hardly escape delusion, which, however, is rather in himself than in those authors.

As a parallel to the passage from Eyrenæus touching the unity or oneness of the *dissolvent* and the *dissolved*, I refer to the following from Plotinus, where he is treating of what he calls the GOOD *or the* ONE. The author supposes the soul properly prepared for the *vision*, which he also speaks of as "*a light acceding to the soul*," and then says: —
"Perhaps, however, it must not be said that he sees, but that he is *the thing seen*, if it be necessary to call these things *two;* i. e. the perceiver [the dissolved] and the perceived [the dissolvent]. But both are one; though it is bold to assert this. Then, indeed, the soul neither sees, nor distinguishes by seeing, nor imagines that there are two things, but becomes as it were another thing, and not itself. Nor does that which pertains to itself contribute anything here. But becoming wholly absorbed in Deity [swallowed up in the Solary Nature, as Eyrenæus expresses it], she is one, conjoining *centre* with *centre*...... Hence this spectacle is a thing difficult to explain by words. For how can any one narrate that as something different from himself, which, when he sees it, he does not behold as different, but as one with himself?"

For a parallel to the expression of joining *centre to centre*, used by Plotinus, I refer again to Eyrenæus, who speaks of the Bodies, meaning Sol and Luna, as being compared by writers to mountains, either because, as he says, they are found in mountains, or by way of opposition: "for, as mountains are highest above ground, so they [the active and passive principles of nature] lie deepest under ground"; and then adds, in his own dialect: —

"But the name is not of so much consequence: take the Body, which is *gold* [man], and throw it into *Mercury*, such a *Mercury* as is Bottomless, that is, whose *centre it can never find but by discovering its own*," &c.

How can any one fail to see that Eyrenæus and Plotinus were treating of the same thing, and that each of them would have man seek the *centre* of the universe in himself, assuring us that, when found, the *dissolvent* and *dissolved* will be known to be ONE? This is that centre which is said to be everywhere, but whose circumference is said to be nowhere; and if a man cannot find it in his own nature, — I do not say in himself as a phenomenal individual, — where shall he look for it? In the nature of another? He will have knowledge of that other nature but through his own nature.

This so-called *centre* has never been named by any word conveying an idea of it, neither has it ever been described or defined so that a mere reader, who is not also a thinker, can obtain any notion of it. It has been called by a word of two letters, as also by words of three, of four, of five, of six, and of seven letters, and by words of many syllables as well as letters. It has been treated of in figures and symbols in infinite ways. Probably no single building in the world would contain the books that have been written about it. It has been called the one, the middle, the equilibrium, the eternal, the unchangeable, the immutable, the self-sufficient, the self-existent, &c., and yet not any of these words serve to make it known; and the moment any name is acknowledged for it, the word becomes " ill-assorted," and its sense passes out of view; and yet this centre remains the sole foundation of philosophy, without which or out of which no man can feel any assured and continued conviction that he has the truth. Most men supply the want of it, when felt, by nerving the will to the performance of certain more or less reasonably supposed duties or ceremonies; and make it a point of conscience to war against whatever brings such a disposition into question; because, indeed, to speak in the language of Alchemy, the *aim* to be right is the white state of the Stone, which, though "incombustible," as the writers say, admits, nevertheless, of a higher perfection, when the *aim* to be right becomes the *right aim;* for then the truth is possessed free from all sense of doubt or struggle, with a sort of infinite or inexpressible conviction that it never has been, and never can be, other than it is; and that whatever does not share it must perish. No man ever had a glimpse of it, who did not feel his whole being carried away by it; and upon such a man all eloquence is wasted, the aim of which is to win him to renounce the vision.

As a still further illustration of the probable meaning of Eyrenæus, I find a passage in Crauford's India, which some may think much to the point. In reference to the philosophy of the Hindoos, Crauford introduces a commentary upon the *Vedanta* school, by Dr. I. Taylor, in which we may easily fancy we see an allusion to the two *Luminaries* of Espagnet, and their unity, to wit:—

"I think we may infer that the philosophy of the followers of the Vedanta school is founded on the contemplation of one Infinite Being, existing under two states or modifications. The first, that of a pure, simple, abstract essence, immovable and quiescent; the second, that of Being displaying motion, or active qualities. Under the first modification he is named Brimh, or *the Great Being*, and Kutasth, or *He who sitteth on high;* under the second, he is named Eesh, *the Lord,* and Jiv, *the Soul;* or, to adapt this explanation to the division already given of these modifications, and to the example by which they were illustrated, we should say that Brimh is Being in its state of simple essence; Eesh is Being exerting energy, and causing the phenomena of the material universe; Kutasth is Being existing in sensitive creatures in its pure, simple state. But perhaps it would be more agreeable to the etymology of the words to call Eesh the principle of energy or power, and Jiv the principle of sensation.

"Everything rests on Brimh, or Being; but to him is more immediately referred Eesh, or power; and to Kutasth is referred Jiv, or sensation."

Here we have the ONE, and *two attributes*, as some moderns have called them; or, nature considered in itself, then *natura naturans*, or nature active, and *natura naturata*, or nature passive; or, in other words, nature as cause and nature as effect. Yet the Hindoo considered all as One, for the comment proceeds as follows: —

"In common books and language, these terms denote separate individual beings; and also in some philosophical systems, Brimh, or Being, and Jiv, that which feels, are considered distinct and different beings; but the Vedantas deny a plurality of *Beings*, and assert that the visible phenomena and sensation are only accidents of one Infinite Being, though, in order to be understood, they speak of them as distinct existences; hence, then, it appears that the Vedanta philosophy is distinguished from all the other systems, by teaching that *the universe consists of one undivided indivisible Being, and motion.* . . . . .

"The reason assigned for attending to these distinctions also corroborates the explanation we have offered. It is not to point out different substances, or beings; but to conduct the mind to the knowledge of that one and all-pervading essence, in which the modifications exist, from which result the distinctions we observe. Unless the nature of these distinctions were understood, the soul must remain ignorant of its own nature [cannot *Know Itself*], and continue for ever under the delusion that it is a sensitive, finite, individual being; but when, by investigating these distinctions, it comprehends the modifications from which they arise, the delusion is dispelled, and it knows itself to be one, *infinite and eternal.* . . . . .

"They who are ignorant of the undivided Being, Brimh, the principle, the impassible one, dispute concerning Jiv and Eesh, the soul and divine spirit; but when this delusion is dispersed, all these distinctions vanish, and there exists only one quiescent spirit."

I hope the reader does not imagine I would refer him to Hindoo philosophy or mysticism for his faith. My object, by such extracts, is simply to indicate a correspondence of thought, by which it may seem probable that the genuine Alchemist had some mode of conceiving all things as *one*, in some sense, and that his speculations had no reference whatever to making gold. Let the student, if he would make trial of their system, first put himself into perfect unity in his own conscience, — let him be absolutely right himself, — and he may then discover in what the distractions of life consist, and in what sense even these make an inseparable part of the true Unity.

I have no wish to recommend these studies, for I very well know that Goethe had his eye upon such speculations in the remark, expressing the most profound experience, that man is not born to solve the problem of the universe, though, he added, he must make the attempt in order to know how to restrain himself within the limits of the comprehensible. Even Eyrenæus has the candor to caution the student not to attempt to practise barely upon his words. Why, then, did he write? Perhaps only to awaken attention and stimulate a curiosity which, though ordinary in its origin, might nevertheless have a divine issue, — as " Saul found a kingdom while seeking his father's asses."

As another parallel I will cite the following: — " It is a certain truth," says Eudoxus, in the Hermetical Triumph, " that, in all the different states of the Stone, the *two* things that are united to give it a new birth come from one sole and same thing; it is upon this foundation of nature that Cosmopolita supports the incontestable truth in our Philosophy, that is to say, *that of one is made two, and of two one; in which all operations, natural and philosophical, are terminated without the possibility of going further.*"

So, Plotinus says, " all things are double, and *the one* is two : and again, *two* passes into one." (Page 467 of Taylor's *Select Works of Plotinus.*)

Two of the principles of the Alchemists are often called extremes, but an invisible one includes the two inseparably, as one idea with two images; or, as we may say, one nature of spirit and matter; or, again, as in the microcosm, one man of Soul and Body.

When the idea is once realized, its illustrations become visible and multitudinous. As a very simple example, in Plutarch's Isis and Osiris, we read that, " wronging and being wronged being two extremes, caused by excess and deficiency, *justice* came by equality in the middle." Justice is the great regulating principle of the universe, operating silently and invisibly, but as surely as it is absolutely beyond the control of man. It is the immovable fulcrum of the balance, — the central point of the magnet with its two poles, neither of which constitutes a magnet by itself.

We may see, also, — whether it has anything to do with the subject or not, — that we have not two distinct senses by which to determine or form an opinion of what is right and what is wrong; but only one sense variously affected. The same sense determines for us what is wrong, which is employed in deciding upon what is right, and if this " eye be dark, how great is the darkness."

Desire, again, is by some said to be the root of all the passions, which are manifested in *doubles*. Thus, joy is desire gratified; sorrow is desire obstructed or defeated: hope is the prospect of gratified desire; fear, the prospect of defeated desire; — and so on for a long train of doubles, the latter belonging to the superficial class, — to excess or deficiency as Plato might say (see the Statesman), — coming and going in time, while the essential remains, in itself invisible and out of relation to time, — a perpetual activity, or *conatus*, as it was formerly called.

But desire and love are almost synonymous terms, for we love and *seek* what we desire, and so also we desire and *seek* what we love: yet neither love nor desire is by any necessary connection directed to one thing rather than another, but either, under conditions suitable to it, may be directed to anything; from which it follows, that it is possible to make God, as the eternal, its object: or, call it truth, and we may see that its fruition must partake of its own nature.

Now, we read, that *it is not common for man to love and pursue the good and the true because they are of this nature; but, on the contrary, and herein lies the great error of life, we call that good which we desire.* From all which we may see that vast consequences depend upon the object of desire, which, as is said, may as naturally be the eternal as the transient, — the attainable and endurable as well as the unattainable and the unendurable, — when suitable conditions exist for it. But here great caution is necessary to guard against merely mechanical, or purely fanciful, theories in dealing with this subject.

I find nowhere in the books of the genuine Alchemists any tendency to mere mechanical theories. One writer dates the commencement of an important advance from his discovering, as he says, that Nature acts magically, and not Peripatetically. Another rebukes a formalist by the question, Can you tell the reason why a lion shakes his tail when he is angry, and a dog when he is pleased?

Another point ought to be mentioned touching desire and love, — that aversion, the opposite of desire, and hate, the opposite of love, are not independent affections, but exist in virtue of desire and love respectively; that is, we do not naturally hate anything in itself, but we hate that which impedes or obstructs us in the pursuit of what we love; and so, in like manner, we are averse to and turn from what hinders us in the prosecution of what we desire. If, then, desire be turned to one only eternal thing, the nature of man taking its character from his leading or chief desire, the whole man is gradually converted to, or, as some think, transmuted into, that one thing, provided we know the true one only eternal thing.

But to know this one only thing is the secret of Alchemy. This I suppose to be that which Plato speaks of as being contained in the smallest compass, which can never be forgotten or lost, but which cannot be learned like other knowledge.

But I have no hope of making that clear to others which is not clear to myself, and my only intention is, by these and the like suggestions, to show *probabilities* as to the real subject of the writers, and that it is Man, or Nature and Man (Sulphur and Mercury), which they would have us understand through or by means of "one only thing," whatever that is, though "it be not very far from any one of us."

I ought to add, having referred to the use of the word *Fire*, that the Alchemists used this word to indicate, among other things, trials of all sorts, to which man is exposed. The writers say of their *Stone*, that it can endure, in this sense, any *fire*, saying, in another sense, that it is Fire itself; for nature, as a principle, cannot be consumed in itself, all of its metamorphoses being superficial and transient, the substance remaining subject only to the power of God, the eternal *conatus* or force by which it exists.

With regard to interpretation in general, the reader will find many useful rules in the Tract by Plutarch, entitled, *How a Young Man ought to Hear, or Read, Poems*, — where examples of poetry are given, drawn from the most ancient poets, with explanations derived from principles of philosophy. But by philosophy we must understand Truth, or, finally, *Nature*. Plutarch, indeed, assumes that his philosophy is true, and then endeavors to "accommodate and reconcile" poetry to it; but we may remember that philosophy itself must be tested by the possibility of nature, and then the rules furnished by Plutarch for the interpretation of poetry will be seen to be applicable to the interpretation of philosophy also, for nature *is*, prior to all philosophies of nature.

Some of Plutarch's rules and applications are so pertinent to the subject I have in hand, that I will recite a few, which the ingenious reader may find applicable in other subjects.

"But of all things," says he, "it is most necessary, and no less profitable, if we design to receive profit, and not injury, from the Poets [the ancient mythological poets are referred to], that we understand how they make use of the *names* of gods; as also of the terms of *evil* and *good;* and what they mean by the *soul,* and *fortune* and *fate;* and whether these words are always taken by them in one and the same sense, or rather sometimes in various senses; and so of many other words."

"Whensoever, therefore, anything is spoken in poems [or any other books whatever, we may add] concerning *gods,* or *dæmons,* or *virtue,* that is absurd or harsh, he that takes such sayings for truths is thereby misled in his apprehension, and corrupted with an erroneous opinion."

In this connection Plutarch quotes: —

> "Joyed was the goddess, for she much did prize
> A man that was alike both just and wise," —

and says, that we are taught by it, that "Deity delights not in a rich or a strong man; but in one that is furnished with both wisdom and justice." "Again," he continues, "when the same goddess (Minerva) saith, that the reason why she did not desert or neglect Ulysses was,

> "'Cause he was wise, and gallant things designed,
> And pondered noble projects in his mind,' —

she therein tells us, that, of all things pertaining to us, nothing is dear to the gods but that wherein we resemble them, to wit, our *virtue;* seeing that *liking is produced by likeness.*"

In another place Plutarch cites a line to the effect that,

"Except what men think such, there's nothing good or ill";

which he says must be corrected by reference to another, thus:—

"But what's so is so, think men what they will."

These two lines express, we may see, the doctrine in Plutarch (as it is also in Plato) stated in the third question of the sixth part of the Symposiacs, to wit, "*That* must first exist which hath no need of any other thing that it may exist; and *that* after, which cannot be without the concurrence of another thing"; for the second of the above lines expresses what is called the substance of things, the first expressing its qualities or accidents, as Aristotle called them. It is worth remarking, that in this unostentatious passage Plutarch has exactly hit off the definitions of *Substance* and *Mode*, by a distinguished philosopher of the seventeenth century, said to lie at the root of his philosophy. The protection of the student against delusion in such definitions is to ask himself what idea he has of *anything*, to the existence of which nothing is conceived as necessary but itself; but he must not look to books for any such idea.

Plutarch quotes:—

> " Of counsel given to mischievous intents,
> The man that gives it most of all repents ";—

and he explains that these lines " are of near kin to what we find in the determinations of Plato, in his books entitled *Gorgias*, and *Concerning the Commonwealth;* to wit, *that it is worse to do than to suffer injury;* and, *that a man more endangereth himself when he hurts another, than he would be damnified if he were the sufferer.*" (Because to be injured is outward, but to injure is a sign of an inward wrong; the one is a surface injury, the other vital, &c.)

Then he quotes:—

> " Seest not how *Jove*, because he cannot lie,
> Nor vaunt, nor laugh at impious drollery,
> And pleasure's charms are things to him unknown,
> Among the Gods wears the imperial crown ? "

And he tells us, that these lines teach " the same doctrine that is found in Plato, to wit, *that the Divine Nature alone is incapable of feeling joy or grief.*"

This doctrine occurs in Plato's Third Letter (to Dionysius), and is stated in Philebus, correctly translated by Taylor, Vol. IV. p. 511, but inaccurately rendered by Burges, Vol. IV. p. 47.

As this doctrine, as stated in Philebus, comes from Protarchus, instead of Socrates, we might consider it as a mere suggestion to be overthrown in the course of the Dialogue; but the same doctrine being stated directly by Plato in the letter referred to, we are at liberty to consider it a definitely formed opinion, and must explain it by reference to the notion previously expressed, of *that* which exists of itself, or *that* to the conception of which no other conception is necessary. This *existence of itself*, as it is sometimes called, is what was supposed without quality, and therefore incapable of either pleasure or pain.

I only refer to this to exhibit Plutarch's mode of illustration.

As different writers used different words for the same thing, as already intimated, and expressed different things by the same word, no general rule of interpretation can be given applicable to all of the writings. Each writing, for the most part, was obliged to be interpreted by itself; but by reading a few of the best authors, and weighing carefully what each one said, *with a constant reference to Nature*, the student might soon begin to perceive to what, in the main, the writers referred, or of what they treated. The next step might have been a sifting of the writings themselves, so as to exclude the worthless and indifferent, the attention becoming confined to some few authors; to which the author of the *Marrow of Alchemy* refers:—

> "But thou of Truth a lover, be advised,
> Beware, and be not easily seduced,
> For be thou sure that all that is devised
> By such, this Art to treat who were induced
>   By envy, is not true; nay, very little
>   In some books, and in some *scarce a tittle*.
>
> "For know this Art a virgin pure remains,
> Though many lovers do her fondly sue;
> She scorns a Sophister, and still disdains
> A breast for to inhabit that's untrue,
>   Yet many press to win the golden fleece;
>   'T is that they gape for as the masterpiece.
>
> "But a true Son of Art doth wisdom prize
> Beyond all earthly good, and his desire
> To it is bent, ne fondly doth devise
> By riches to ambition to aspire;
>   His studies all to knowledge are inclined,
>   Prizing alone the riches of the mind."

The books being sifted, and a few only retained, — such as the *Hermetical Triumph;* Artephius (in Salmon's *Clavis Alchymiæ*); Espagnet's *Arcanum; The Open Entrance to the Shut Palace of the King;* Ripley's *Compound of Alchemy,* but more especially *Ripley Revived,* by Cosmopolita; *The Marrow of Alchemy; Zoroaster's Cave; Aurifontina* (a small volume, containing fourteen treatises, including the excellent letter of Bernard Trevisan to Thomas of Bononia); Sandivogius; Pernety's, or Gaston le Doux's *Dictionary,* both valuable; Basil Valentine; Isaac Hollandus; and some other works, not forgetting those of Hermes, whose *Smaragdine Table* is said to contain the whole Art, though comprised in a page or two; — the books being sifted, I say, the student, after passing through various transitions of confidence and doubt, prizing the books highly and verging upon a contempt for them, may finally be content to use them as means only, and, having his attention directed to one only thing, may at last strike the key-note which reduces to harmony all discords: and then, some of the writers say, he may burn his library; for the Truth is prior to the books expressing it, and remains unaffected by all the perversities of man in the treatment of it. The Art cannot be false, however men err about it, so these writers say; and when discovered, it is found to be true in all countries, under all governments, and in view of all religions.

The awe with which all of the writers approach the subject is very remarkable, and their unwillingness to write openly of it seems to be of a Pythagorean character. They seem to understand also that contemplation and controversy cannot keep company; for though the latter may sometimes sharpen one's wits, it always disturbs the balance, the judgment, whose equipoise is so necessary in all cases, but especially in a student of nature. Hence the recommendation of Espagnet in taking leave of his reader, already recited: —

"Farewell, diligent reader: in reading these things, invocate the spirit of Eternal Light; speak little, meditate much, and judge aright."

THE END.